CW00471308

COMMANDANT
OF THE
TRANSVAAL

The Life and Career of
General Sir Hugh Rowlands, VC, KCB
1828-1909

W. Alister Williams

bridge
books
Wrexham

First published in Wales
in 2001
by
BRIDGE BOOKS
61 Park Avenue
Wrexham
LL12 7AW

ISBN 1-872424-41-4

A CIP entry for this book is available from the British Library

Printed & bound by
MFP
Manchester

Contents

Illustrations and Maps

Lt. General Hugh Rowlands, VC, CB.

Introduction and Acknowledgments

The Victoria Cross, Britain's highest decoration for gallantry in the face of the enemy, has always held a fascination for the general public since it was first awarded to men who had served in the Crimean War. Hugh Rowlands of Llanrug, north Wales, was one of those early recipients and the first Welshman to gain the award. Today, he is all but forgotten in the village of his birth and his only memorial (other than his gravestone) is to be found in Cardiff in the Museum of the Welch Regiment where his decorations and other artefacts form the central part of that regiment's Crimean War display. Occasionally, his name appears in print when his service in South Africa during the period 1878–9 is glossed over, often disparagingly, as part of a wider military history of that country. This short biography attempts, for the first time, to record the full details of Hugh Rowlands' military service and to clear some of the 'fog' that surrounds the controversial period in South Africa.

Hugh Rowlands was not a typical Victorian officer. He did not come from a military background, nor was he English or the possessor of great wealth. Rather, he was the son of a minor Welsh landowner who served in the British Army as a professional soldier at a time when the term professional was something of an alien concept. He gained great distinction as a fighting soldier and as an administrator. His career was a full one, enabling him to rise to the very top of the military tree and yet, when he came up against the élitism of the 'officer corps', his career very nearly came to an abrupt end.

My grandparents, who purchased Sir Hugh's home after the death of Lady Rowlands, knew that he had been awarded the Victoria Cross but had no other knowledge of his career. My research began from personal interest and not with the intention of publication. In 1992, the private publication of a limited number of copies of this work, met with some approval and I have been encouraged to expand that work and make it available to a wider public.

I am indebted to a number of individuals and organisations for their generous assistance with the research for this book and I have endeavoured to record all their names below. If I have overlooked anyone, I offer my sincere apologies.

The Museum of the Welch Regiment, Cardiff; the National Army Museum, London; the National Library of Wales, Aberystwyth; the Museum of the Border Regiment, Carlisle; the Gwynedd Archives Service; the Library, University College, Bangor; the India Record Office, London; the British Library, London; the National Maritime Museum, Greenwich; the Public Record Office, Chancery Lane and Kew; the Library of the Royal United Services Institute, London; the Bodlian Library, Oxford; the Museum of the South Wales Borderers, Brecon; the Museum of the Staffordshire Regiment, Lichfield; the Killie-Campbell Africana Library, Natal; the Natal Archives Depôt; the Transvaal Archives Depôt; the late Lt. Bryn Owen, RN (Retd); Mr David Christie-Murray; Mr Christopher Bacon; Mr H. W. Kinsey; Mr Ron Lock; the late Mrs Rosie Hughes; Mr Ken Williams; Mr John Winton; Mr Colin Moynahan; Mr Philip Gon; Commander Haly, RN (Retd); the late Brigadier Guy Gough, DSO, MC; Mrs Diana Pym; Mr Donald Morris, Mr David Clammer; Mrs Mary Lloyd Williams.

W. Alister Williams
Wrexham
2001

Chapter 1
A Welsh Background

The parish church of Llanfihangel-yn-y-rhug stands on a hill about half a mile from the village of Llanrug to which it gave its name. Although it is claimed to be of sixth century foundation, no one is very certain when a church was first built on this site and any documents which may have helped trace its early history have long since fallen victim to the ravages of time. To attempt to write a history of the parish would be difficult for many reasons, not least of which being the fact that most of the major events of the past seem to have passed it by or, at best, cast their influence upon it only as something of an afterthought. It would appear that the area was always impoverished, situated as it is on the edge of the mountains, on the margin of cultivation.

From the hills above the village an observer can look to the west and see the island of Anglesey stretching towards the horizon and, if fortunate, can see the turrets of the mighty fortress of Caernarfon, down on the edge of the Menai Strait. To the east the outer sentinels of Snowdonia rise steeply, bleak and cold in their winter covering of snow and hardly any more hospitable in their summer garb. The mountains are given over almost exclusively to the occupation of rearing the hardy Welsh mountain sheep who somehow manage to locate sufficient pasture on the moorland and between the lofty crags. In many ways, the local population has much in common with the sheep for they too were historically a rather isolated community which for centuries managed to eke out a precarious living on the side of the mountains but, despite their hardships, rarely strayed far from their birthplace. They are a people who are still rather suspicious of outsiders in the same way that island communities tread carefully when dealing with newcomers from the mainland, and are immensely proud of their own way of life and culture. They have never been prosperous, not even when the slate industry was expanded in the late eighteenth and early nineteenth centuries which, although it certainly brought employment to the area, omitted to bring with it any great wealth; that went elsewhere.

A few individuals from the parish have, over the years, managed to stand out from their fellows and carve a small niche for themselves in the story of Llanrug. Men such as William Owen, Prysgol who began life as a farm servant with no formal education but who became a musician of renown, composing hymns such as *Bryn Calvaria*, and writing a number of books which went into several editions and who ended his days as a prosperous farmer. David Thomas, better known as Dafydd Ddu Eryri, the outstanding Welsh poet of the late eighteenth century, lies buried in the churchyard as does Humphrey Edwards, physician on the frigate HMS *Tamer* which circumnavigated the world under the command of the poet Byron's grandfather. To this short but illustrious list of famous sons must be added one other who, during the relatively brief span of one lifetime, succeeded in linking Llanrug to the far flung corners of the British Empire, a local boy born and bred, who brought honour, glory and a great deal of pride to the community and to Wales.

Hugh Rowlands, the second son and third child of John and Elizabeth Rowlands was born on 6 May 1828,* at the family home, Plastirion, a substantial house located about half a mile from the parish church of Llanrug. His father was a member of the minor county gentry and was the heir of Hugh Rowlands of Ty Mawr, Llandwrog, steward to the estate of the local magnate, Lord Newborough. The Rowlands family claimed descent from Bleddyn ap Cynfyn, the 11th century Prince of Powys and, indirectly, from Llywelyn Fawr, Prince of North Wales. All the evidence that has survived about the family's origins would appear to bear out this pedigree although there is no absolute documentary proof.

One ancestor, John ap Rowland of Plas Nant, Betws Garmon, assumed the anglicised surname of Rowlands after leaving Wales during the second half of the seventeenth century. A romantic account of his early

---

* *All the military records show Hugh Rowlands as having been born in 1829, and his eventual retirement from the army was based upon his having reached the maximum age allowed for a general officer. The parish records of Llanrug, however, show him as having been baptised in 1828. As there are entries in the register immediately after his it would appear that the year of baptism is correct and therefore all other records are based upon an inaccurate recollection of his year of birth.*

life is given by John Jones (Myrddin Fardd), in *Llen Gwerin Sir Gaernarfon*, taken from the writings of Owen Williams (Owain Gwyrfai of Waunfawr) whose mother was reputed to have been born at Plas Nant.

> A gentleman by the name of John Rowlands left his home in Nant … and went to London as a shopkeeper. In 1666, during the Great Plague, the owner of the shop where he worked died. John Rowlands was stricken with the disease but recovered. He inherited the property plus all the shop owner's money. He was then called upon to look after other shops, and as the owners died of the epidemic, John Rowlands inherited their properties and their wealth.
>
> John Rowlands decided to return home to Nant. He packed a ship sailing to Caernarvon, with his silver, gold and furniture, but the ship disappeared and was never seen again. His remaining treasures were packed and carried by sledges from London to Nant.
>
> With his newly acquired wealth, John Rowlands, on his return, was able to build 'Plas-y-Nant', in 1667, and buy land around his home in Betws Garmon.[2]

In reality, John Rowlands had established himself as a banker of some repute in Lombard Street, London. Upon his retirement, he returned to Caernarfonshire and the family home at Betws Garmon.* He married Frances Owen (grandaughter of the Royalist Major General Sir John Owen of Clenennau) and they had eleven children (including two sets of twins). His children were to marry into the notable families of Baron Hill, Beaumaris and Brogyntyn, Oswestry. Richard Fenton mentions John Rowlands in a short inventory of paintings held at Plas Llanfair — 'A fine Portrait of old Rowlands of Nant by Sir Peter Lely. He was the Post Office Palmer[4] of his day, and had a place in the foreign Post Office'.

He built Plas Nant in 1671 and, for the remainder of his life, enlarged his estate by the purchase of numerous properties in various parishes in central Caernarfonshire which included land in the parishes of Betws

---

* *The oldest surviving building at Plas Nant is the large stone structure now known as The Chapel. There is ample evidence to suggest that this dates from the period before the estate was inherited by John Rowlands and that it might well have been used for domestic purposes. It is likely, therefore, that this was the original home of the Rowlands family. In the woods at Plas Nant is a carved stone recording that John Rowlands liked to sit there, away from the bustle of life.*

Garmon, Clynnog, Llanwnda, Llandwrog, Llanllyfni, Nantlle and Llanbeblig. He also owned the summit of Yr Wyddfa (Snowdon). He served as High Sheriff of Caernarfonshire between 1688–89 and 1692–93 and as a justice of the peace. He died in March 1703, aged 58, and was buried in St Garmon's Church, Betws Garmon.

John's brother William was also an entrepreneur of some standing. His career as a cattle drover was typical of that of many aspiring Welshmen up to the end of the nineteenth century. Being a cattle drover had considerable status within a community. Today, in an era of mechanised transport and refrigeration, it is difficult to appreciate the importance of the drovers who annually moved tens of thousands of cattle (and other livestock) from the farms of Wales to the markets of England. During the Civil War, Archbishop John Williams described the trade as '... the Spanish fleet of North Wales, which brings hither what little gold and silver we have'. In Caernarfonshire, the local population was almost entirely dependent upon the sale of their animals in distant markets and the drovers, as their trusted representatives, had to be men of good character. All such men had to be licensed by the Quarter Sessions, aged over thirty, married and householders. The law stated that, in the event of financial problems arising, they could not be declared bankrupt in order to rid themselves of any financial obligations which they may have to individual farmers.

Financially, a successful drover could hope to do very well and it would appear that William Rowlands became a wealthy man. It must be more than a coincidence that he should have been a drover at the time when his older brother was a banker. The dangers of carrying large sums of money on the return journey to Wales were well known and gangs of thieves were commonplace. To overcome this problem the money was often deposited in a bank in London and some form of bill of exchange carried back to the farmers in Wales who could cash it at a local banking office. This practice became commonplace in later years and provided the foundation of several of today's joint stock banks but it would appear that the Rowlands' brothers were amongst the first to introduce such a system into their dealings in order to safeguard both themselves and the small farmers in Caernarfonshire.

William lived at Cryg in the parish of Llanfairisgaer and, with the wealth generated by his business, purchased land in the nearby parish of

Llanrug which, by the end of the eighteenth century, amounted to an estate of over 1200 acres. It seems likely that the family moved to live in a house named Nantalgwyn in Llanrug but that some time during the eighteenth century moved about half a mile away to a property which they named Plastirion. The house at Nantalgwyn was probably demolished and the stones and other architectural features re-used in the new house. Today, nothing remains of Nantalgwyn other than a rough outline of the property in a field which still bears the name. William's son greatly enhanced the family's property by his marriage to his cousin, Jane Hughes of Bodaden, and by the beginning of the nineteenth century, Plastirion had become a noted residence in the area and the Rowlands family highly respected.

William Rowlands' great grandson, the above mentioned Hugh of Ty Mawr, earned the lasting enmity of the villagers of Llanrug when, in partnership with Mr Assheton Smith of Vaenol, he enclosed the common land in the parish, gaining 450 acres in the process. Until well into the twentieth century, he was remembered as the man who had 'stolen the common land from the people'; indeed, such was the ill feeling at the time that a troop of dragoons had to be billetted on the village for six months to maintain the peace. Hugh was a captain in the Royal Carnarvon Militia and served as High Sheriff of the county in 1807–8. He died in 1830 when the estate passed to his nephew, John Rowlands, who was already living at Plastirion with his wife and three children. John was very much associated with public service and, in addition to being deputy lieutenant, a high sheriff (1832–3), a justice of the peace and a captain in the Militia, he served as steward to the Llanfair-Brynodol estate and was an active participant in local affairs.

It was into this secure, middle class and strongly Welsh environment that the future general was born and throughout his life, during which he spent many years away from Wales, he maintained his links with his homeland, spoke the language of his ancestors until his death, included his Welsh royal background on his heraldic arms and longed for his beloved Plastirion. He was proud of being a Welshman and, whenever possible, associated himself with all things Welsh.

Much of Hugh Rowlands' formative years are a mystery as no records have survived before September 1837, when he enrolled as a boarder at Beaumaris Grammar School on the island of Anglesey, where his brother

Beaumaris Grammar School, Anglesey.

John was already a pupil.[7] The regulations of the school stipulated that new pupils must have had a basic classical education before entering and it is probable that Hugh had received such training from his uncle, the Reverend Hugh Rowlands, MA, who held the living at Llanrug from 1834 until his death in 1843. If the extant records are to be believed, Beaumaris provided very little beyond the continuation of this classical education and even such basic subjects as English grammar and mathematics appear to have been beyond the scope of the curriculum. Hugh lodged with the headmaster of the school, a man who appears to have had a considerable influence upon his early life and whom he later acknowledged as his mentor. He remained at the school until 1842 when, due to a lack of documentation, his activities again become a mystery.

By 1846, he had reached a decision about his future career and applied for a commission in the army. This choice was not unusual for a young man in his position in the mid-nineteenth century. Being the second son of a small estate, he was expected to find his own way in life as, on the death of his father, the estate at Plastirion would undoubtedly go to his brother. The ancient English inheritance rule of primogeniture would have made any thoughts he may have had about inheriting the family property little more than wishful thinking.

Having no family connections with the army (apart from his family's service with the Militia and a very distant kinsman, Hugh Rowlands Williams, killed whilst serving in Grenada), the route to a commission would have to be by purchase. Traditionally, persons wishing to be commissioned were required to pay a fixed fee for the rank (see Appendix I) which had been set by the Horse Guards (the office of the Commander-in-Chief) in 1821. All applicants had to be over 16 years of age and had to be accepted as suitable by either the Commander-in-Chief himself or by the colonel of a regiment for which the applicant hoped to be selected. If his name was approved, it was placed on the waiting list until such time as a suitable vacancy occurred. This wait could be very short, if the candidate had influence, or very long if he had little or no support. It was accepted that aspiring junior officers would canvas for support from those whom they felt might have some influence to ensure that their names were not overlooked. Some candidates were commissioned without purchase but these were the exception rather than the rule and, in the period 1834–38, fewer than 25% of new commissions were by non-purchase entry. It is interesting to note that, in the selection of non-purchase entrants, '… in no case, are the personal merits of the applicant considered for one single moment.'

Hugh Rowlands was in need of sponsors and between 1846 and 1849, his family sought out support from within society in Caernarfonshire, beginning with such dignitaries as Lt. Colonel Douglas Pennant of Penrhyn Castle and Mr Bulkley-Hughes, MP. They appear to have met with little success and the net was cast wider. His brother John was, by the late 1840s, practising as a solicitor in Chester and, during a visit to that city in December 1847, Hugh was initiated into the Cestria Lodge of the Order of Freemasonry. By special dispensation as he was only 19 years of age and the normal minimum age was 21. Why he decided to join such a distant lodge is not evident until one examines the membership list which included Field Marshal Viscount Combermere, a hero of the Peninsular Wars, who agreed to support his application. In 1849, when at last the way seemed clear for his entry into the army, Lord Fitzroy Somerset (later to become Lord Raglan), in his capacity as Military Secretary at the Horse Guards, introduced a new regulation whereby all applicants for a commission had to pass a formal examination to show that they had attained an acceptable level of education. This would be carried out by the professors at the Royal Military College, Sandhurst, and covered history, geography, algebra, logarithms, Euclid, French, Latin, field fortification, orthography and caligraphy. Recognising no doubt that it was some years since he had left school, and that he was no longer accustomed to any form of academic testing, Hugh went to London and was enrolled at Mr John Taylor's Cramming Academy at Woolwich, an establishment which specialised in gaining young gentlemen an entry into the army. Within a month, in August 1849, Hugh had sat, and passed, the entrance examination and was offered an ensigncy[13] in the 53rd Regiment of Foot (the Shropshire Regiment). For some unrecorded reason, this offer was changed almost immediately to that of an ensigncy* in the 41st Regiment of Foot (The Welch Regiment) and was hastily accepted.

On 25 September 1849, Ensign Hugh Rowlands' name appears, for the first time, on the muster roll of the 41st, which was then stationed at Cork, Ireland but he does not appear to have joined the regiment in person until New Year's Day, 1850.

The regiment remained in Ireland until February 1851 when it was posted to the Ionian Islands in the Mediterranean and, shortly after his arrival at Corfu, Hugh Rowlands was promoted to the rank of lieutenant — without purchase. His replacement as ensign would have paid for the commission and Hugh's father would therefore have recovered the capital outlay involved in gaining the original vacancy. Shortly before Christmas of the same year, Hugh returned to Britain on leave and then rejoined the Regimental Depôt in Ireland where he remained until November 1853 when he was posted back to the regiment which was, by then, stationed on Malta. There he was placed in the Grenadier Company, an appointment which was to have profound effects in the future. Shortly afterwards, the 41st was ordered to prepare for a posting to what was probably the most unpopular station in the Empire, the West Indies, where disease always took a heavy toll of both officers and men. Before the posting was effected however, the orders were changed, and the regiment was told to hold itself in readiness for active service.

---

* *An ensign was the infantry equivalent of 2nd Lieutenant.*

Chapter 2
An Officer and a Gentlemen

What type of army was it that Hugh Rowlands joined in 1849 at the age of 21?

To the British public as a whole, the army was ... an unknown institution. Most of the soldiers were ... serving overseas. Their presence at home was not particularly noticeable. And when they were seen in Britain on parades or on guard-mounting ceremonies or on manoeuvres, they were objects of distant admiration. Their presence was welcomed, provided it was at a distance. Closer contact was less acceptable. There were occasions, perhaps all too frequent, when civilian society totally rejected the military — as when a soldier was prevented from riding in an omnibus, or when three sergeants were expelled from a box in Her Majesty's Theatre in the Haymarket because they were wearing the uniform of the British Army.
[*The Army in Victorian Society*, Gwyn Harries-Jenkins]

Since the time of Napoleon, the armies of the Continental powers had developed into societies in their own right with their own code of conduct and a social cohesiveness. They viewed professionalism and the development and understanding of technology as highly desirable. They were becoming modern, industrialised armies; forces adapted to a world which was changing around them. In France and Prussia, performance and honour were all that mattered. In Britain, the army was almost unchanged from that which had fought at Waterloo, indeed Lord Raglan, who was appointed to command the army sent to the Crimea in 1854, had last seen action in 1815 and still felt nervous when in the presence of French forces! In the British Army, it was tradition and history that was foremost in the minds of the high command and it was generally believed that officers should come from a level in society where education, manners and habits were paramount; that men of distinction must come, by definition, from the higher echelons of society. The British public, irrespective of their social background, respected and admired officers who served in regiments stationed peacefully at home while frowning upon officers who saw action while serving with the East India Company army in the far flung corners of Empire. After all, the élitist and class structured British army had defeated the meritocratic French army during the Napoleonic Wars. But was this not a sham? Had Wellington won the battle of Waterloo despite the inherent weaknesses in the British army rather than because of them? There is no evidence to support the theory that the British aristocracy and gentry were braver or more altruistic or honourable than any other class of society. They saw themselves as serving their country, but were they not perhaps simply serving themselves? For many, a military career was short term, a means of filling in some time until the individual concerned was in a position to take up his true vocation as an administrator of a large estate. It would make an interesting research project to discover the percentage of the most successful high ranking officers who were also the heirs to large fortunes as opposed to those who were the second or third sons. This latter group, with no great inheritance to rely upon, were, of necessity, compelled to develop a military career, to become professional in their chosen vocation. Certainly, a high proportion of the leading military names of the nineteenth century were drawn from this second category, men such as Wellington, Raglan, Gough, Roberts and Wolseley.

The British officer class drew its members from a narrow band of society, the landed gentry. True, there were officers who had begun their careers in the ranks but they were very much the exception that proved the rule. Occasionally a non-commissioned officer was commissioned as a reward for distinguished service but, unless he was from a gentlemanly background, he would usually only be commissioned into an unfashionable regiment and, even then, his career would be unlikely to advance much further. For every Sergeant Luke O'Connor, VC[2] who rose through the 76th and 23rd Regiments of Foot to Major General and

---

* Sergeant Luke O'Connor of the 23rd Regiment of Foot (Royal Welch Fusiliers) was awarded the Victoria Cross for his gallantry at the battle of the Alma in 1854 and was commissioned into the same regiment. He eventually retired as Major General Sir Luke O'Connor, VC. Even in this case, however, everything was not at it would seem on the surface. O'Connor had an affluent medical sponsor and it would seem that he could easily have obtained a commission at the start of his military career.

a knighthood, there were dozens like Sergeant Ambrose Madden, VC[3] who rose through the ranks and was commissioned into the 2nd (and later the 4th) West India Regiment and died of fever in Jamaica with the rank of lieutenant.

Army society merely reflected the civilian society within which it was based. Just as the lower classes deferred to their 'betters' in civilian society, so their military counterparts accepted the inborn right of their officers to command and lead them on the parade ground and in battle. By the mid nineteenth century, British society had undergone a dramatic change with the growth in status of the middle classes. The new industrial society which was imposing itself more and more upon all aspects of British life, had created a new strata in society, that of self-made men who were the captains of industry. They had taken hold of the industrial towns and cities and, with their excess wealth, had spread their power to rural society where they were able to purchase great estates or use their money to buy themselves into the great landed families of the aristocracy. This change was reflected everywhere but in the military. There, the upper classes still held sway, possibly because the rising middle classes saw no profit in military service and made little effort to challenge the status quo.

There was an inherent fear of military power among the political leaders of British society. Ever since Cromwell had removed the will of Parliament and imposed martial law under the generals in the seventeenth century, every effort had been made to ensure that another military coup could not occur. By maintaining an officer class that was based upon an individual's position in landed society, it was felt that the danger of military interference in politics could be averted. However, in reality, the British army was far from being apolitical. If the political structure of the country was geared towards retaining power in the hands of the landed aristocracy and gentry, then the officer corps, which was drawn from that very social class, would be highly unlikely to take any action that could be seen as prejudicial to their future inheritance. This being so, the 'officer corps' actually helped to maintain the status quo, in itself a political action.

---

* *Sergeant Ambrose Madden of the 41st Regiment of Foot (The Welch Regiment) awarded the Victoria Cross and commissioned for his gallantry at Little Inkerman in 1854. He died in 1863.*

This type of military society was maintained very simply. Entry into the army was dependant upon either patronage or purchase and, more often than not, on both. The granting of a military commission was almost a formality to the higher echelons of the ruling classes, the sons of dukes, earls and lords and, even if a commission had to be purchased, it was of little significance to families that had unearned incomes running into tens of thousands of pounds per annum. The purchase system was, however, the primary impediment to the greater professionalism of the army. As Trevelyan wrote:

> The large and important class of well-educated young men who depended for their advancement upon their own exertions, and not upon their wealth and connections and who constitute the pith of the Law, the Church, the Indian Civil Service and other active professions, are thus ordinarily excluded from the Army.

Once a young man had purchased his initial rank of ensign or cornet* all that outlay could be recovered on his next promotion and the sale of his vacated position to an aspiring candidate from the same social order. The system of purchasing commissions was not therefore one designed to raise funds for the army, the War Office or the officer corps. It was, rather, a simple, but highly effective, system of regulating entry into the 'club' — by making a charge that was sufficiently high to make it impossible for the lower classes to gain a place on the first step of the ladder and to deter those slightly higher up the social order from considering the army as a future career. Each potential promotion was also governed by the same two factors of patronage and purchase so that any individual who did manage to slip through the net encountered the same obstacles at every stage of advancement. If a 'border-line' case were to purchase his way into an ensigncy then there was a period of time available for reflection when 'betters' could consider his suitability for enhancement and, if he were found lacking in any of the required social standards, financial impediments could be placed in his way.

For an young man from Hugh Rowlands' background the path of a career as an army officer was unlikely to be a smooth one. Although far from being a member of the 'lower order' of society — the Rowlands estate brought in an income of over £1,000 per annum — he was not a natural member of the inner circle from which officers were drawn. In terms of potential patronage, he was on very weak ground for his background gave little indication of a natural, hereditary military ability and there was no one that would immediately come to mind as a personal sponsor or referee. Although the family mixed in the local society in Caernarfonshire, this was very much a social backwater, located some 250 miles from the hub of society in London. There is no evidence that any nineteenth century member of the Rowlands family had any involvement with the capital before Hugh's journey there in 1849 to further his education. Both Hugh and his brother John had been educated locally at Beaumaris Grammar School, which would hardly serve them as a social asset in the years to come. When Hugh was called upon in later life to provide details of his education he merely referred to Woolwich — with the unstated implication that it was the Royal Military Academy at Woolwich rather than a few weeks spent at a cramming establishment — and omitted to mention Beaumaris at all. Finally, neither Hugh nor his brother gained entry to that other great social milieu, university. Their life had centred around north west Wales and, until John set out to carve his own career as a lawyer in Chester (which, as we have seen, was also to prove to be a key factor in Hugh's future career prospects), there was little to suggest that they would move beyond the limited social circle of Caernarfonshire. Like their ancestors for over a hundred years, it was anticipated that they would remain minor landowners, hopefully marrying well and thereby enhancing their assets by the purchase or acquisition of further property.

Once accepted for a commission in the army, an officer was obliged to pass through further processes of social vetting before commencing upon his career. The military arm which he would be called to serve in was, as with everything else, very much dependent upon his social background. The army was divided into four major groups, the Household Division (comprising the various regiments of Foot and Horse Guards) which stood at the top of the ladder and to which entry was restricted to a very chosen few who could not only fit in with the expensive nature of regimental life but could also fit in with the social obligations of life in London society. Rarely in times of peace were the Household regiments posted overseas, or indeed outside the capital. Secondly, there was the technical corps such as the Royal Artillery and the Royal Engineers which required, even in the nineteenth century, a level of academic training and natural intelligence that was far in excess of that attained by all but very few of the officer intake of the army, but which carried little social status. Thirdly, there were the cavalry regiments with their own internal pecking order: maintaining a string of horses added an additional financial burden to any prospective officer's family which eliminated another layer of potential entrant. Finally, there were the regiments of the Line, the infantry. Within these there was an unwritten but clearly recognised pecking order with regiments such as the Royal Fusiliers and the Rifle Brigade carrying far more status than such lowly units as the 41st Regiment. In all branches of the army the social pecking order was clearly visible to all by the percentage of officers with titles serving in any particular regiment. This distinction between regiments was further reflected by the official prices charged for commissions into different regiments and arms. In 1821, a coronetcy* in the Household Division, cavalry or infantry, would cost £1,200, in the dragoons £840 and in the regiments of Foot £450. Yet further evidence of the manner in which wealth and disposable income was used to maintain the élitism of the officer corps.

Hugh Rowlands is known to have been passionately fond of horses throughout his life and a very proficient horseman and yet appears to have made no attempt to enter a cavalry regiment. Undoubtedly, the reason for this was his social position in civilian life which was reflected by his being commissioned into the 41st Regiment, which had little or nothing to do with personal choice or indeed with the fact that he was a Welshman. The ranks of the 41st, although the regiment was designated 'The Welch Regiment' was composed mainly of Irishmen (as were indeed most British regiments at the time) who saw military service as an escape from the poverty of their homeland.

Few officers could financially afford to remain in the junior ranks for any length of time. Army pay was insufficient to enable them to live according to the social norms of the Officers' Mess. In most cases their military salary had to be supplemented from private means and, unless their family was financially solid, this could not be maintained indefinitely. To provide the state of financial happiness outlined by Mr Micawber in *David Copperfield*, an officer had to both gain advancement through the ranks (so that his income would match his necessary

---

* *A cornet was the cavalry equivalent of 2nd Lieutenant.*

expenses) as well as seek additional sources of revenue such as voluntary active service. Extended periods of peace could prove fiscally disastrous as there was always the great danger of an individual being placed on half-pay, often for several years.

For Rowlands, and other young men in a similar position, the army was not to be a temporary means of passing a few years until he came into his inheritance, it was to be a full-time career. As far as he could see, there was little likelihood that he would ever inherit the Plastirion estate or even a substantial share of it. Without such a prospect, and with no professional qualification to fall back on, it would appear obvious that his way in life would have to be made through the army and that if he were to become financially independent he would have to progress quickly. Throughout history, young men who have sought to make their name and fortune in a military career have always tried to position themselves at the sharp end of army life. Of the many thousands of junior officers in the service of the Crown, only a very few would make it to the higher echelons of the army and a sizeable proportion of these would do so by patronage. For those young men who, like Hugh Rowlands, had no natural patron to whom they could turn to for preferment, there was only one way forward, they had to gain the attention of their military superiors which would, hopefully, lead to their advancement. It is little wonder that talented young officers such as Wellington, Wolseley, Roberts, Gough, without any major claim to patronage, gained their reputations early as men of action, serving in campaigns in India or the Peninsula. It was only after they had successfully made their way up the first few steps of the career ladder that they were able to obtain positions where their mere presence was in itself sufficient cause for them to be noticed. There was always an element of manipulation in the development of a successful career but, even more important, there had to be a liberal portion of luck, of being in the right place at the right time. There can be few better opportunities for a junior officer than that offered by active service in a war zone. Since 1815, the British army had gone through an extended period of peace in Europe, the only campaigns were in the far flung corners of the empire. It was Hugh Rowlands' good fortune that the European peace was about to come to an end and all the complex pieces of the career jig-saw that was to set him on the road to success were to fall into place quickly.

Chapter 3
The Crimea

Throughout the nineteenth and twentieth centuries, Russian foreign policy was centred upon her need for an all-year-round warm water port. Although the Russian Empire was by far the largest single land mass in the world under the control of one central government, its access to the sea was restricted to a number of northern ports which could not be used during the winter due to ice. The ports on the Black Sea were, for all practical purposes, land-locked as in order to sail out of that sea it was necessary to pass through the narrow Bospherous and Dardenelles, both sides of which were under the control of the decaying Turkish Empire.

The Turkish Sultan ruled an area which, in addition to the Middle East, also included south-eastern Europe, traditionally a potential powder-keg of unrest. In 1829, Greece had won her independence from the Turks after a bitter struggle lasting five years, an event which heralded a period of renewed activity amongst other vassal nations in the region. In 1850, a religious dispute broke out over who should be responsible for retaining the keys to the Christian holy places in Jerusalem. The French, as champions of the Roman Catholic Church, insisted that the catholic monks should have the privilege and this caused friction between them and the Greek Orthadox Church. The French threatened the Turks with military action until, in December 1852, the latter agreed to their demands. This decision incensed the Tsar of Russia who saw himself as the protector of the Orthodox Church and, when trouble broke out in Montenegro during which a Turkish force took action against christians, he lent his support to the Austrian Empire which was demanding the full withdrawal of all Turkish forces from the area. It was clearly pointed out to the Sultan that a refusal to comply with the Tsar's wishes would be seen as sufficient grounds for a declaration of war between their two empires.

Britain, who had strong interests in the eastern Mediterranean, saw this threat of war as a concealed attempt by Russia to dismember the Turkish Empire and thereby increase her influence in the region. Such a scheme, if successful, would pose a direct threat to Britain's naval power in the Mediterranean and would have to be opposed with the utmost vigour. There followed a dual of wits between the British and Russian ambassadors in Constantinople, with Britain coming down clearly on the side of the Sultan. When France, without consultation with any of the powers involved, sent her fleet to the region, the Tsar adopted an even more entrenched position and insisted that the Russian government had the right to act as the protectors of the Greek Orthodox Church. The Sultan refused to make any changes to his country's policy and, on 21 May 1853, before any further consultations could take place, the Russians broke off all diplomatic relations with the Turks. Ten days later, they issued an ultimatum giving the Turks eight days in which to meet their demands, otherwise the Tsar would order his army to cross the frontier. Very politely, the Turks refused to comply and, on 2 July Russian troops entered Moldavia and Wallachia. Britain, France, Austria and Prussia all appeared to be in support of the Turks and the Royal Navy was sent to join the French fleet off Gallipoli. Austria, as Turkey's nearest neighbour, was expected to take the initiative against Russia but did not do so and it was Britain and France who made the first move in support of their new found ally. Their fleets were moved to Constantinople in readiness to enter the Black Sea should all the diplomatic endeavours fail to reach a peaceful solution. Message followed message to and fro across Europe, but neither side was prepared to back down and, in the end, the dispute boiled down to the simple fact that Russian forces were on Turkish soil and were refusing to withdraw. With his subjects clamouring for action the Sultan had no alternative other than to declare war which he did on 5 October 1853.

As the year drew towards its close, the British and French fleets remained inactive at Constantinople and the arrival of news of Turkish victories in the Danube region greatly heartened the local population as honour appeared to have been satisfied and there was the hope that peace might be restored in the coming year. The arrival in Constantinople of a British steamer in a battered condition changed the situation dramatically. The vessel had been part of a small Turkish naval squadron which had taken shelter in the port of Sinope on the southern coast of the Black Sea. They had been surprised at anchor by a much larger Russian fleet and, in the ensuing conflict, all the Turkish warships were sunk with a loss of over 4,000 men, while the Russians claimed to have lost only 1 officer and 33 sailors killed and 230 wounded. It was not the naval defeat, nor the scale of the destruction which horrified the Turks and their allies but rather the manner in which the Russians were reported to have systematically killed all the survivors who were struggling in the water after the loss of their ships. It had been agreed by both sides that a truce would exist between their naval forces and the Tsar had personally declared that it was his intention to confine military operations to the Danube region. The attack on Sinope was therefore seen as a clear indicator of the Russian contempt for the principles of war – the fact that reports stated that the Russian ships came across the Turkish squadron by accident, and that the first shots had been fired by the Turks, was carefully ignored.

As early as December 1853, the First Lord of the Admiralty had put forward the suggestion that the Black Sea port of Sebastopol should be destroyed. During the first week of January the British ship HMS *Retribution* sailed into Sebastopol Bay and conducted a survey of the approaches to the port and its defences. In the subsequent report which was sent to London, Captain Drummond highlighted the fact that the entrance to the harbour could easily be blocked by the Russians and that only a land based assault could achieve any measure of success. This opinion was also reached by Lt General Sir John Burgoyne (Inspector General of Fortifications and Commander of the Royal Engineers). By February, the French Emperor had concluded that an assault on Sebastopol was unaviodable and passed this decision on to Lord Raglan when the latter passed through Paris en route to take up his command in the eastern Mediterranean.

The French government persuaded the British Cabinet to support them in issuing a warning to the Russians that any further acts of aggression would result in military action being taken by them and demanded that all Russian warships should be recalled to their base at Sebastopol. A message to this effect was sent to the Tsar on 12 January and, as a consequence, five weeks later Russia broke off diplomatic relations with both countries whilst agreeing to strive for a peaceful solution to the problem. On 27 February, an ultimatum was issued stating that, unless Russia withdrew all her forces from Turkish territory, Britain and France would declare war. The Tsar chose to ignore the threat and war was declared on 27 March and, four days later, the first of 10,000 British troops embarked from Malta.

The 41st Regiment of Foot had received their orders to stand-by for active service on 3 March and, between then and their embarkation, they passed the time training with the new muzzle-loading Minie rifle which had been issued to only 26 men but which all men were given practice in the use of in order to save time when sufficient numbers of rifles arrived to equip the whole regiment. The regiment was brigaded with the 47th and 49th Regiments under the command of Colonel H. W. Adams, CB, of the 49th.

On 10 April, the regiment embarked aboard the steam transport *Himalaya* bound for Gallipoli in Turkey but, en route, their destination was changed to Scutari on the Bospherus where, after five days at sea, they disembarked and were quartered in the Turkish barracks (which were later to become infamous as the Scutari Military Hospital). The brigade of which the 41st was a part of was, at this time, designated the 2nd Brigade of the 2nd Division, the whole formation being under the overall command of Sir George de Lacy Evans, but there seemed little hope of any offensive action in the foreseeable future.

The first anti-British shots of the war were fired on 13 April when HMS *Furious* was bombarded by shore batteries while trying to evacuate the British and French consuls from Odessa and, three days later, Admiral

SS Himalaya, *the troop-ship that transported the 41st Regiment to Turkey.*

The full dress uniform of a captain of the Grenadier Company of the 41st Regiment.

Dundas retaliated by bombarding the Russian defences with a 900-gun broadside. This was continued until 22 April, leaving substantial casualties in the Russian city,

The weeks passed slowly for the soldiers at Scutari where the 41st, like the other British regiments, was champing at the bit as news arrived that the Turks were fighting the Russians on the far side of Bulgaria. The days were occupied with visits to other regiments and to the local settlements but the novelty of such distractions had worn thin by the time the last of the British infantry arrived in Turkey at the end of May.

On 3 June, the regiment moved out of the barracks and into a tented camp, a move which cannot have been objected to as many reported that their former accommodation had been infested with fleas. Their stay under canvas was short lived and, two weeks later, they embarked as part of an Allied force which was bound for the city of Varna on the Bulgarian coast, where they were to act as a reserve for the Turkish army which was still in action further north. Any hopes that they might see action themselves were soon dashed and the soldiers settled into a routine of relative inactivity, moving occasionally from one camp to another whilst the Turks succeeded in halting the Russian advance. By the end of the month, the enemy was withdrawing north and it appeared that the war was over bar the diplomatic moves which would undoubtedly take many months. The 41st, however, was not to escape from Bulgaria without loss for, on 6 July, it moved into a camp at Yursakova where an outbreak of cholera occurred. There being no facilities whatsoever for dealing with the disease, several Welchmen were amongst the 500–600 British soldiers who died as a consequence.

In addition to the health problems, the British army was also encountering difficulties with the supply of rations, and the situation in the 2nd Division was particularly bad. As if these were not problems enough, the British camp had been devastated by a hurricane on 2 July. All in all, the situation was deteriorating and did not auger well for a successful military campaign conducted so far away from home, solely dependant upon the sea for the re-supply of the troops in the field.

In London, the British government had already decided to assault Sebastopol and public support for such an action was being driven on by the press, not least *The Times*. Peace may well have appeared possible but, in the capitals of the Allied nations, the clamour was for war. The Russians had to be taught a lesson to ensure that the problems which had led up to their war with Turkey did not reappear once they had recovered from their military reverses. On 29 June the Prime Minister, Lord Aberdeen, notified the Queen of the Cabinet's decision to order an attack on Sebastopol and to send additional troops to join the force under Raglan's command. The decision may have been very clear cut but the wording which was sent to Varna was, if not ambiguous, at least indecisive. Aberdeen wrote to Raglan that the decision was 'pressed very warmly and recommended to be taken with the least possible delay' and that the final decision would rest with Raglan, St Arnaud (the French commander) and Omar Pasha (the Turkish commander). To a military commander, the 'gentlemanly' nature of political correspondence prevalent during the nineteenth century left much to be desired; while leaving the final military decision to the man on the spot, it also created a candidate for the role of scapegoat should things go wrong. Indeed, there is strong evidence to suggest that had Raglan declined to take part in any invasion of the Crimea, he would have been replaced as commander of the British force. The 'Eastern Question' had plagued European foreign ministries for many years and the time seemed ripe to resolve the problem, once and for all. In London, if anyone had been unclear of what was taking place in the east, it was all made crystal clear when *The Times* suggested that the Allies should invade the Crimean peninsula,

... and permanently settle in our favour the principal questions in dispute ... those objects were to be accomplished by no other means, because a peace which should leave Russia in possession of the same means of aggression would only enable her to re-commence the war at her pleasure.

Preparations for the invasion, such as they were, went ahead with all possible speed and in the 41st Regiment, Captain Goodwyn was promoted to Major and the vacant captaincy, and command of the Grenadier Company, was purchased by Hugh Rowlands. This was a significant appointment for the young officer as the Grenadier Company, along with the Light Company, of any line regiment were seen as something of an élite unit and made up of men who were usually of above average physique and who displayed good martial qualities. To take command of such a company was in itself something of an honour.

Chapter 4
Battle of the River Alma

Originally scheduled to sail from Varna on 15 August, the Allied fleet was delayed by adverse weather conditions until the end of the first week of September. Nearly four hundred vessels of all types made up the armada which presented an imposing sight whether clearly visible in daylight or outlined by the numerous lights displayed at night. The weather settled and the ships sailed north, up the Bulgarian coast, to the island of Fidonisi where they linked-up without incident. From there they sailed east and carried out a prolonged reconnaissance in order to select a suitable place to disembark on the Crimean coast.

At daybreak on 14 September, they anchored near a location known as the Old Fort, some 20 miles south of Eupatoria and 30 miles north of Sebastopol. There were no enemy forces in the area (according to reports, some of the local population regarded the invaders as a force come to free them from the Russian yoke) which meant that the landing could go ahead unopposed and for three days the boats ferried the 27,000 British, 25,000 French and 8,000 Turkish soldiers and their equipment to the shore. The 41st Regiment landed on the first day with Hugh Rowlands and his company disembarking from the *City of London*; in total the regiment had a strength of 25 officers and 930 NCOs and men, each of whom had to carry as much as possible on his person as it would be several days before other supplies could be landed, sorted and issued. One anonymous eye-witnesses account gives a vivid description of the scene on the beach, reminiscent of a carnival atmosphere:

> By twelve o'clock in the day, that barren and desolate beach, inhabited but a short time before only by the sea-gull and wild-fowl, was swarming with life. From one extremity to the other bayonets glistened, and red coats and brass-mounted shakos gleamed in solid masses. The air was filled with out English speech, and the hum of voices mingled with loud notes of command, cries of comrades to each other and an occasional shout of laughter. Very

amusing was it to watch the loading and unloading of the boats. The officers of each company first descended, each man in full dress. Over his shoulder was slung his haversack, containing what had been, ere it underwent the process of cooking—four pounds and a-half of salt meat, and a bulky mass of biscuit of the same weight. This was his ration for three days. Besides this each officer carried his great-coat, rolled up and fastened in a hoop round his body, a wooden canteen to hold water, a small ration of spirits, whatever change of underclothing he could manage to stow away, his forage cap, and, in most instances, a revolver. Each private carried his blanket and great-coat strapped up into a kind of knapsack, inside which was a pair of boots, a pair of socks, a shirt, and, at the request of the men themselves, a forage cap; he also carried a water canteen and the same rations as the officer, a portion of the mess cooking apparatus, firelock and bayonet of course, cartouche box and fifty rounds of ball cartridge for Minié, sixty rounds for smooth bore arms. The beach was partitioned off by flagstaffs, with colours corresponding to that of each division, in compartments for the landing of each class of man and beast.

On reaching the beach, the 41st remained there until late afternoon when they marched to their allotted camping site. Basic equipment, such as tents, had not been brought ashore with the men and very soon conditions began to hint at what was to come in the months ahead. Hugh Rowlands wrote in a letter home:

> We started and marched about four miles, arriving on the ground when it was dark; drizzly rain having fallen for the greater part of the morning, we were wet when we got there, and in the middle of the night it came down in torrents, and without fire or anything in the shape of creature comforts, we passed a miserable night lying huddled together in a ploughed field, inches deep in mud. The following morning, luckily was fine and when the sun came out we got alright again.

On 19 September, the armies began their march towards Sebastopol. The British force marched on the left of the Allied advance with the French and Turkish forces positioned between them and the sea. Raglan ordered his infantry to march in two columns, the left column comprising the Light, 1st and 4th Divisions and the right column the 2nd and 3rd Divisions, marching alongside the French. The good spirits with which the march began soon gave way to depression as men began to collapse from the combined effects of tiredness, heat and cholera. The men were allowed to leave behind their knapsacks and to carry only those items that were deemed essential in their blanket rolls.

As the Allied armies, numbering some 60–65,000 men, reached the Bulganek river in the early afternoon of the first day of the march, Russian horsemen were spotted on the far bank. These were followed by infantry and the Allied forces were formed into line in readiness. The anticipated first action then commenced when Russian artillery opened fire and the British artillery replied at which point the enemy force was seen to retreat and, shortly afterwards, the Allies crossed the river where they set up camp for the night.

On the second day of the march the armies approached the river Alma where, as the high ground on the far side of the river was held by a strong enemy force in prepared positions, it became clear that the first major action of the campaign would take place.

The Russian commander's decision to defend the line of the river Alma was a wise one. On the northern side of the river (which was only some 40 feet wide and very shallow) the bank sloped gently to the water's edge, but the south side was formed by a steep slope, rising to 500 feet above sea level, crowned by a rocky cliff, broken only by a few very narrow tracks. The Allied armies had to approach the crossing from the north and any attempt to remove the Russians from their positions would therefore mean a frontal assault up the slopes, the least favourable form of attack which, if the defences were conducted competently, gave little promise of success.

Reconnaissance parties brought in detailed reports of the river crossing. Commencing at the coast (on the Allied right) there was a sandbank at the estuary which would enable troops to cross the mouth of the Alma. One mile up-stream was the village of Almatamack where the river could be crossed by means of a ford which gave access to a rough road leading up the steep southern side of the valley. For a further mile, the river banks were given over to vineyards and gardens until a white farmhouse was reached where there was a second ford and track leading towards the Russian positions. Vineyards then continued for another mile where there was a third fording point and track leading from the village of Bourliouk. A quarter of a mile further upstream, the main Sebastopol–Eupatoria road crossed the river by means of a wooden bridge. The river and the high ground on the southern bank created a form of amphitheatre overlooking the Allied position with Kourganie

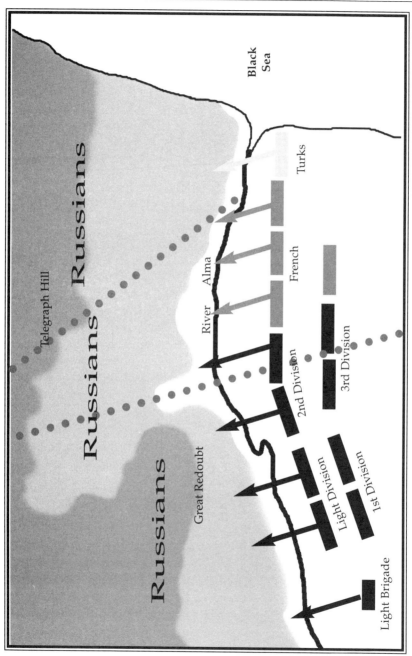

Battle of the River Alma

Hill (450 feet) in the east and Telegraph Hill (400 feet) in the west. Between these two hills there was a plateau which dropped down towards the river which could only be accessed by scaling a steep bank which varied from 10 to 15 feet in height. This small cliff would be difficult for infantry to scale at the best of times and would serve as an insurpassable obstacle to horses and horse-drawn vehicles and guns. In reality, the Russian position on the heights overlooking the Alma was perfect for defence. The task facing the Allied armies, particularly the British, was one that most generals would have done much to avoid.

The British force halted about a mile short of the river, with the French on their right filling the two mile gap between them and the sea. The original plan, which was drawn up by St Arnaud on the evening of the 19 September, entailed the French 2nd Division and the Turkish force moving off at 5*am* the following morning towards the two most westerly crossing points of the river. The remainder of the Allied forces would stay in camp until 7*am* when they would begin to cross in front of Telegraph Hill, Kourgane and Bourliouk. The French would then turn the Russian left while the British turned their right before the main attack was sent in in the centre.

In the morning, St Arnaud discovered that Raglan had no intention of following what the former thought was an agreed plan of action. At 7*am* there was no sign of movement from the British camp and it was not until thirty minutes later that Raglan's headquarters were reported to be on the move, a delay caused by the difficulties which he had encountered in manoeuvring his forces from the defensive position which they had been compelled to adopt during the night. The baggage train had to be protected and the gap between the British and French armies closed — Raglan, an experienced Staff Officer, left very little to chance if it could be avoided. Eventually, at 8*am*, the army began to advance towards the river. The first shots were fired at the Russian positions at about 10.30*am* by warships acting in support of the French on the right. By 11.30*am* the advance was ordered to halt about $1^1/2$ miles short of the river, at the top of the northern slope.

A brief conference between Raglan and St Arnaud resulted in the modification of the plans so that the flank attack of the French right would seize the area of Telegraph Hill before the British commenced the more difficult frontal assault on Kourgane Hill.

At 1*pm*, the forces re-commenced their advance towards the river. The 2nd Division was positioned to the rear of the village of Bourliouk and, when the order to advance was given, the 41st moved forward until they came within range of the Russian artillery at which point they turned sharply left. The movement was performed in the style of Waterloo, forty years earlier, which was where most of the senior commanders had last seen active service. The regiment moved in open columns by sections and, such was their training, that when it wheeled into line again, it was in perfect order, despite the heavy fire coming from across the river. A further sharp turn was made and then the regiment was instructed to lie down to allow the Allied artillery to fire at the Russian batteries over the heads of the men. Rowlands wrote:

> The nearer the Alma was approached, the more plunging was the fire. I believe all our loss was from artillery, and so plunging was the fire that I saw the head of a rear rank man shot off without touching the front rank man.

Again, the 41st was ordered to advance only to be halted a short distance from the now burning village of Bourliouk. This relative inactivity and inability to return the enemy's fire due to the range involved, when added to the dense smoke coming from the nearby houses, placed a severe strain upon the men, many of whom had never previously been in action. General Sir George Brown, commanding the Light Division (on the left of the 2nd Division), failed to realise that the Alma flowed at an angle across his front and therefore took no steps to compensate for it. As a consequence, his right was beginning to overlap the 2nd Division's left and there was the potential for chaos, compounded by the poor visibility resulting from the burning village and surrounding area.

At 2*pm*, about an hour after the advance had begun, and probably in order to rectify the error of Sir George Brown, the 41st was ordered to move to the right and, with the 49th Regiment, they emerged from the smoke in columns of four, reforming into line before reaching the river bank. In later years, Rowlands recalled his feelings as he waited to go into action for the first time: his nerves began to affect him and he felt butterflies in his stomach. Suddenly, he heard a voice call out in Welsh from somewhere in the rear, 'Rwan yr hen Blastirion! Rwan am biff!' ['Now old Plastirion! Now for a fight!']. It was a man named Lovell who came from Tan-yr-allt, Llanrug and who was also serving in the regiment. The realisation that he was being watched and that the honour of his family was at stake, caused him to calm himself for his first taste of the realities of war.

Rowlands led his men across the river at the most fordable point and, once on the far bank, reformed them in a small ravine at the foot of the slope. So far, the regiment had not fired a single shot. Suddenly, for no apparent reason, a Russian battery which was in a position to inflict terrible damage on the British troops that had crossed the river, retreated and its position was quickly overrun by the men of the Light Division. This piece of luck enabled the 41st and 49th Regiments to continue their advance up the slope, bayonets fixed, almost unhindered. The Russians, in the dense formations which they had adopted, were an easy target and heavy casualties were inflicted upon them by the advancing British infantry. Slowly, they began to abandon their positions and the advance was able to continue until the men of the 2nd Division were able to link up with the French who, having swept around the Russian left wing, had seized Telegraph Hill. The Russians were now in full retreat and the first action of the campaign was an Allied victory. Rowlands described the advance of his men up the slope:

> We advanced in double column of companies from the centres of divisions, with artillery on our flanks, and a strong line of skirmishers in front of all. On nearing them we deployed into line; the men remarkably steady under a heavy fire of shot and shell from a battery on a high hill … the 41st right wing joined with the French left, and all did their job admirably, driving them from their position in four hours and a half.

That evening, three companies of the 41st were detailed for picket duty whilst the others rested but, despite the withdrawal of the enemy, the death toll for the Alma was not yet complete as during the hours of darkness a number of men, who had survived the perils of the day unscathed, died of cholera. The next two days were spent attending to the wounded and the opportunity for a rapid advance on Sebastopol, while the enemy's forces were in disarray, was allowed to slip through the hands of the Allies. They were to pay dearly for their tardiness.

Following a meeting at the camp near the river Belbec during the evening of the 24 September, it was decided that the Allied forces would not launch a direct attack from the north against the Russian city. Instead, a flanking march to the east would be made which would bring them onto the weakest side of the city and also enable them to capture ports through which supplies could be brought by the Royal Navy. This decision was the direct cause of the campaign turning from one of movement to a stagnant trench and siege warfare which was to last for a year.

The line of march adopted by Lord Raglan was from the Belbec, south-east towards Mackenzie's Farm, Tractir Bridge, the valley of the Tchernaya, Kadikoi and then to Balaclava, a small port in the south of the Crimea. Much of the route would be through heavily wooded countryside. At one point there was a strong possibility of the column running across a Russian army moving out of Sebastopol but the march passed uneventfully, mostly due to the advent of thick fog. Had Raglan avoided any delay at Balaclava and immediately moved his forces north-west towards Sebastopol he could have taken over the positions on the left of the Allied line but, instead, those positions went to the French and, as a consequence, Inkerman and Balaclava came under the British sphere of operations. In addition, the British force would have to guard the route to and from Balaclava, hold the right flank of the Allied line and play a full role in the anticipated assault on the city of Sebastopol. It was stretching their men and resources beyond that which could be regarded as being reasonably possible.

By 4 October, the 2nd Division was placed on the right of the British line, encamped on the Heights of Inkerman which (with the benefit of hindsight) was to prove to be the most dangerous position of any held by the the Allied forces. The high land was covered with brushwood and had steep slopes leading down to the river Tchernaya. A deep ravine ran north-westwards towards the Russian positions and the nature of the ground made any hope of speedy assistance, should it ever be necessary, very difficult. Sir de Lacy Evans realised that the situation of his division was precarious and made as many preparations as possible to meet any attack in this area. His plans were hindered by the absence of large numbers of his men who were drafted into working on the construction of a 21-gun battery some two miles away. By 17 October, the Allied gunners were ready and at 6.30*am* the bombardment of Sebastopol was opened by the 126 guns already in position. It was envisaged that such a bombardment would soon reduce the city's defences to such an extent that an assault could be carried out without excessive casualties. The

Russians however, became the masters of repair and each night made good the damage inflicted during the day. Rowlands wrote:

> But dawn disclosed a new factor. At nightfall we had looked on works reduced to shapeless heaps, on ruined batteries and disabled guns. Before morning the parapets had been rebuilt, the batteries repaired, and fresh guns from the inexhaustable supplies of the ships and arsenal had occupied the embrasures; and the Allies could now begin to realise how formidable was the opponent who could thus as chief engineer, wield the resources of the place. The recuperative powers of the enemy, taken along with the failure of the French batteries, diminished indefinitely the chance of the place being taken by assault. Nevertheless, the hope of achieving that result was far from being abandoned.[6]

On 25 October, the situation took a turn against the Allies when the British force in the valley above Balaclava was forced to fight for its survival and the small success achieved by the Russians made the position of the Allies far more precarious. On the day following the battle of Balaclava, the pickets of the 2nd Division, under the command of Major Eman of the 41st, were posted as usual when, at about noon, reports were received that large numbers of Russians were moving up the slope towards their position. Advancing in three columns, the Russians (estimated at some 6–7,000 men) were met with accurate artillery fire as soon as they came within the range of the British guns and were forced to retire. Sir de Lacy Evans then ordered the regiments under his command to advance in pursuit of the enemy and, because of the nature of the terrain, all semblance of military precision quickly vanished and small groups of officers and men became involved in numerous skirmishes before the Russians withdrew behind their defences at Sebastopol with losses which were estimated to have been well in excess of 200 killed and 80 men taken prisoner, whilst the 2nd Division lost 9 men killed and 4 officers and 58 men wounded. The British units involved in this action, which came to be known as Little Inkerman, were the 30th, 41st, 47th, 49th and 95th Regiments with the 55th in reserve. Among the four companies of the 41st that became embroiled in the fighting was the Grenadier Company led by Captain Hugh Rowlands.

It now became obvious to the Allies that the Russians were preparing for a major confrontation before the assault on Sebastopol could be launched and measures were therefore taken to meet such an attack if, and when, it came. Pickets were placed in more advanced positions in order that earlier warning might be given of any enemy movements, reconnaissance parties and night patrols were increased but, apart from a greater intensity of the Russian bombardment of the Allied positions, no extraordinary activity was recorded.

Chapter 5
The Battle of Inkerman

The night of 4/5 November was cold and wet. The hot, disease ridden days of the Crimean summer, which had provided such a good breeding ground for the spread of cholera, were giving way to the first touches of winter. On the heights above the ruins of Inkerman the British Army slept protected as usual by a ring of pickets, the men of the Light Division guarding Victoria Ridge and Careening Ravine, the pickets of the Guards Division on a prominence looking north along Careening Ravine and the 2nd Division pickets on the Heights of Inkerman itself. As the night advanced, the dampness changed into a fog which clung to the ground in the numerous ravines and slowly made its way up the slopes onto the higher ground.

The most advanced picket on the Heights was that of the 95th Regiment, positioned on Shell Hill, under the command of Captain Vialls. The position was a miserable one and afforded its occupants no protection from the elements and they were delighted when, in the early hours of 5 November, Major Goodwyn of the 41st, who was Field Officer for that area, ordered them to withdraw down to the foot of the south-eastern slope of Shell Hill, where they found a more sheltered position. This move, coupled with the dark and the advancing fog, caused a great deal of confusion amongst the soldiers making up the picket and, in consequence, Captain Vialls ordered the withdrawal to continue as far as the Old Post Road so that they might regain some semblance of order.

Between 2 and 3am, several of the picket positions had reported the sound of wheels carrying up the slopes from the direction of Sebastopol. It would appear that, without exception, the officers who received these reports paid little heed to them, assuming the sound to be coming from some innocent source. Lieutenant Ward of the 47th Regiment crawled forward beyond Shell Hill and, on his return, reported that the noise was coming from British ammunition wagons which were moving up to the artillery batteries. Major Bunbury of the 23rd Regiment, positioned further on the British left, came to the conclusion that the sound was that of Russian ammunition wagons moving up to the batteries protecting the city. Suspicions were not even aroused about an hour later when the bells in the distant city began to ring; those that heard them recalled that it was Sunday and placed no significance on the unusually early hour.

At a little before dawn, the men who were to make up the day pickets, paraded for inspection in the camp of the 2nd Division. The Officer of the Day for the 2nd Brigade of the 2nd Division was Lieutenant Colonel William O'Grady Haly of the 47th Regiment who later recorded the events which followed:

> ... the Picket of the Second Division paraded on that part of the Inkerman Road running through the camp of the Division. I proceeded in Command of the Picket forming the line of advanced posts from the road or Shell Hill to the Ravine running between the 2nd and Light Divisions, the most advanced Picket being under the brow of Cossack Hill near the Ravine.

As dawn began to break over the valley of the Chernaya, one of the pickets of the Light Division, comprising an officer and about 30 men, saw what they thought to be British troops approaching them out of the fog. Too late, they realised their mistake and they were captured without a shot being fired. On Shell Hill, the advanced picket commanded by Vialls, and accompanied by Major Goodwyn, was relieved by the Grenadier Company of the 41st, commanded by Captain Hugh Rowlands and Lieutenant William Allan. The relieving picket was also accompanied by Lieutenant Colonel Haly who was informed by Major Goodwyn that all was quiet and that nothing unusual had been observed during the night.

> The tents of the Second Division are pitched on the verge of the plateau which we occupy, and from the right flank of the camp the ground rises gently for two or three hundred yards to a ridge covered with scrubby brushwood, so thick that it is sometimes difficult to force a horse through it. These bushes grow in tufts, and are about four feet in height. On gaining the ridge you see below you the valley of the Tchernaya, a green tranquil slip of meadow, with a few white houses dotting it at intervals, some farm enclosures, and tufts of green trees. From the ridge the hill-side descends rapidly in a slope of at least 600 feet high. The brushwood is very thick upon it, and at times it is almost impervious. At the base of this slope the road winds to Inkermann, and thence to Sebastopol.

In a letter home, Rowlands described the scene as his men assumed their duties:

> When I passed through the night picket you cannot imagine a more cheerless aspect. I halted the company about half way up and went to plant sentries about one hundred and fifty yards over the hill.

Rowlands had therefore resumed the occupation of the position which had been evacuated by Vialls during the night and was situated on the highest point in the area. Evidently all was still quiet and the advancing Russian force still remained undetected by any of the pickets — any firing which would have occurred on the two forces making contact would have been heard by Rowlands and his men. Both Lieutenant Colonel Haly and Lieutenant Allan confirmed Rowlands' later report that all was quiet. The Light Division pickets were certainly not engaged at this time as is borne out by the histories of the regiments involved and the report of *The Times* correspondent William Howard Russell:

> It was a little after five o'clock when Brigadier-General Codrington, in accordance with his usual habit, visited the outlying pickets of his own brigade of the Light Division. It was reported to him that 'all was well' and the General entered into some conversation with Captain Pretyman, of the 33rd Regiment, who was on duty on the ground, in the course of which it was remarked that it would not be at all surprising if the Russians availed themselves of the gloom of the morning to make an attack on our position, calculating on the effects of the rain in disarming our vigilance and spoiling our weapons. The Brigadier ... turned his pony round at last, and retraced his steps through the brushwood towards his lines. He had only proceeded a few paces when a sharp rattle of musketry was heard down the hill and on the left of the pickets of the Light Division. It was here that the pickets of the Second Division were stationed.

The credit for detecting the Russian advance lies fairly and squarely with the pickets of the 2nd Division and, indeed, with the Grenadier Company of the 41st Regiment. Lieutenant Allen wrote:

> We had just taken up our day position, and posted our sentries when ... our left sentries shouted that 'The Russians are in front'. We had no more than time to get under arms, and extend the main body of the picket, when shots were exchanged, and the enemy advanced up the slopes in dense masses, preceded by skirmishers...

The firing which then commenced was undoubtedly that heard by

Codrington's men and it told the Russians that, at last, their attack had been detected. A few more minutes would have taken them within striking distance of the British camp but, even without them, a rush up the slope would carry them through the thin line of pickets and on towards the still sleeping or barely awake Allied camp.

Rowlands' own description matches that recorded by Allan but adds more detail :

> ... I returned to the company, which had just piled arms, and ordered the men to take off their packs, when the sentries commenced firing in a most determined way. I ran up to enquire the cause, when one shouted that there were columns of Russians close to them. I stood to my arms and advanced in extended order, thinking it was a sortie something like that on the 26th ... On getting to the top of the hill, I found myself close upon, very truly, thousands of Russians. I immediately gave the order to retire, which was done for about 200 yards, when I halted on the next bit of high ground [a continuation of Shell Hill where the right of this picket linked up with the pickets of the 1st Brigade] and lay down, quietly waiting for them. Fitzroy [Lieutenant G], who was in support of me, then came up with the Light Company. His men I likewise extended to reinforce my own. When we retired the Russians came on with the most fiendish yells you can imagine. We commenced firing. To my dismay I found that half the flint-locks missed fire, which dispirited the men. At this period the Russian columns opened with their field pieces, pouring in grape and shell. We then got some reinforcements of the 55th and 30th, but we were gradually obliged to retire ... I begged and entreated Colonel Haly to allow me to charge, which he did ... and after a little hand-to-hand work we turned them and drove them back about 500 yards, when we were met by a fresh column, who compelled us to retire.

In this account of the opening round of the Battle of Inkerman, Rowlands omits to mention the gallantry which he exhibited during this charge on the enemy ranks. Lieutenant Colonel Haly continued the story:

> ... as soon as our bayonets told on the foremost of the enemy they turned back up the hill toward the heavy columns which now showed on the brow. In leading that charge, the first of the day, being somewhat ahead I got surrounded by Russians, & was bayoneted off my horse ... the Russians then bayoneted me on the ground and disabled me.

Haly's situation was critical. On losing his seat on the horse the officer's foot had become caught in the stirrup and he sustained a very

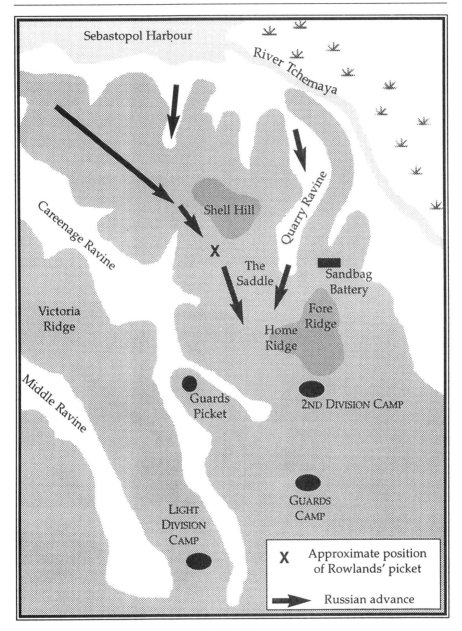

Battle of Inkerman

heavy fall. He had already sabred three Russian soldiers in the charge and expected the worst as, like all other British soldiers, he had heard rumours that the Russian troops killed any wounded men that they came across. As the grey clad soldiers surrounded him he could see only a grisly end.

> … a bayonet thrust grazing my left shin bone, left leg, and coming through the thick of the calf. Another small prod in the back and the thigh. A probe in the ribs and a thrust in my face which grazed my temple … My life was providently saved.

Rowlands had seen what had befallen Haly and, accompanied by Privates McDermond and Kelly of the 47th, he rushed to his assistance. Forcing their way through the advancing Russians they reached the

Private McDermond of the 47th Regiment saving the life of Colonel Haly during the battle of Inkerman. McDermond was awarded the Victoria Cross for this action. [Loyal Lancashire Regiment Museum]

disabled officer and were involved in a short but very fierce struggle during which Kelly was killed and Rowlands was severely wounded in the arm. Despite this, Haly was lifted up and carried back to the comparative safety of the British lines. The colonel was to survive his injuries and gave the full credit for saving his life to Rowlands, McDermond and Kelly. He later wrote to Goodwyn of the 41st who recorded the contents of the letter:

> Colonel Haly has informed me that Captain Rowlands behaved very gallantly on this occasion and that he considers that he owes his life to him. Also that Captain Rowlands exerted himself very much in holding the ground occupied by his advanced picket as long as possible that morning against superior numbers of the enemy.

Haly also wanted to show his gratitude to Rowlands in a more practical manner and wrote to Lieutenant General Pennefather, recommending that the gallant captain be promoted immediately to Brevet Major. Pennefather replied that he had anticipated the recommendation and had already urged such an award with Lord Raglan and had high hopes that the nomination would very soon be acted upon.

The correspondent of *The Times*, William Howard Russell sent a vivid description of the fighting home to his newspaper:

> Then commenced the bloodiest struggle ever witnessed since war cursed the earth. It has been doubted by military historians if any enemy have ever stood a charge with the bayonet, but here the bayonet was often the only weapon employed in conflicts of the most obstinate and deadly character. ...The battle of Inkerman admits of no description. It was a series of dreadful deeds of daring, of sanguinary hand-to-hand fights, of despairing rallies, of desperate assaults —in glens and valleys, in brushwood glades and remote dells, hidden from all human eyes, and from which the conquerors, Russian or British, issued only to engage fresh foes
>
> The Second Division in the centre of the line, were hardly pressed. The 41st regiment, in particular, were exposed to a terrible fire, and the 95th were in the middle of such disorganising volleys that they only mustered sixty-four men when paraded at two o'clock. In fact the whole division numbered only 300 men when assembled by Major Eman in rear of their camp after the fight was over. The regiments did not take their colours into the battle, but the officers nevertheless were picked off wherever they went. Our ambulances were soon filled, and ere nine o'clock they were busily engaged in carry loads of men, all

The battlefield of Inkerman. Shell Hill is directly in the centre with Sebastopol in the distance on the right.

covered with blood, and groaning, to the rear of the line.

The intensity of the hand-to-hand fighting at Inkerman went down in British military history. One member of the 41st wrote home about the death of Lieutenant Colonel George Carpenter:

> Our poor colonel was shot in the thigh, and when down a Russian shot him in the back, clubbed his musket, and struck him on the mouth. These Russians are more barbarous than the Burmese, and it is but little quarter our men will give them the next time they meet, for they all vow a deadly vengeance, and it is not to be wondered at. But to the poor colonel. I saw death in his face when he was brought in at half-past twelve, and I told him I feared he would fight no more ... he was a fearless soldier and a kind-hearted man, and I am proud to have been considered by him as his friend.

There was no further mention of Rowlands' activities during the fighting at Inkerman and it would therefore seem likely that the wound which he had received necessitated his leaving the field to receive medical attention. He was treated for three days by the medical services in the Crimea and, on 8 November, was taken aboard a ship at Balaclava bound for the hospital at Scutari.

After Inkerman, the pickets of the 2nd Division received some criticism for their failure to detect the Russian advance sooner and some even hinted that they were guilty of negligence. Those who knew the true circumstances rushed to their defence at that time and again later, when the war was over and the same attacks were made in the press which was publicly analysing the whole Crimean shambles. One such attack appeared in the *Morning Herald* on 7 January 1857, in an article about General Codrington. Haly who, as Field Officer of the Day, had overall responsibility for the pickets on that eventful morning, wrote personally to Codrington:

> I must distinctly state that no alarm was given either on my right or left flank, as must have been the case if the outposts of the Light Division had been first engaged. The first shots fired on the morning of the 5th November at Inkerman were those of the advanced sentries of the Grenadier Company of the 41st regiment which, as on all occasions, behaved in the most gallant manner, under the distinguished Captain Rowlands ... the pickets under my command were not ... surprised, taken or driven off the ground.

There can be little doubt about the gallantry displayed by Rowlands and his men that morning and, to his brother officers who were there at the time, he became 'the man who started the Battle of Inkerman'.[13] Later, when the authorities established the Victoria Cross as the highest of all awards for gallantry in the face of the enemy, it was his action on 5 November which earned Hugh Rowlands a place in the history books as the first Welsh recipient.

Chapter 6
The Siege of Sebastopol

The Allied commanders in the Crimea had confidently anticipated that Sebastopol would fall shortly after the bombardment of its defences had begun in the autumn of 1854. The Russian attacks at Balaclava and Inkerman and the ability of their engineers to repair the damaged defences, quickly destroyed this hope but not before it was too late for the Allies to make adequate preparations for the winter. The story of the mismanagement of the British logistics by the authorities in Britain and by the commissariat in the field is well known and this is not the place to re-examine the problems. Suffice it to say that the winter of 1854/5 was particularly severe, even by Crimean standards, and the troops who were encamped outside Sebastopol suffered terrible privations due primarily to the gross inefficiency of those in authority who were, by comparison, living in luxury.

When it was realised that offensive operations against the city of Sebastopol would have to be postponed until the following spring or summer, arrangements were made for a more permanent and efficient deployment of the Allied armies. The British force was divided into two sections, the Right Attack (covering the plateau which lay between the Woronzoff Road and the Dockyard Ravines), which covered about half a mile and focused its attention on the Russian defensive works known as the Redan and the Malakov, and the Left Attack (covering the area from the Woronzoff Ravine to the Picket House Ravine) which also covered about half a mile of front. Late in 1854, the French agreed to assume the responsibility for any assault upon the Malakov and thereby left the British to focus their attention upon attacking, and capturing, the Redan.

Just over five weeks after Inkerman, on 18 December, Hugh Rowlands rejoined the 41st in the Crimea and resumed command of the Grenadier Company which had been under the temporary command of Lieutenant

The 41st Regiment in the rifle pits before Sebastopol, 1855.

William Allan. The regiment had lost its commanding officer, Lt. Colonel Carpenter, at Inkerman and was now under the command of Lieutenant Colonel Eman. Its main duties were to furnish pickets for the Allied perimeter, a duty which came round every fourth or fifth night and, because of the severe cold, it was common to find officers making applications to go before medical boards with a view to returning to Britain; those who had been wounded were in a particularly good position to have their request granted. There is, however, no evidence that Rowlands ever made such an application; in fact, he appears to have been the only wounded officer to return to the regiment from Scutari throughout the period of hostilities. It seems that he actually sought active service.

During January, the 41st went into the trenches on the Right Attack for the first time where they were to serve until the fall of Sebastopol nearly nine months later. The conditions in which they existed, as described by Captain Graham, would have been familiar to a generation of British servicemen in the fields of France and Flanders some sixty years later:

Camp of the 2nd Division before Sebastopol during the winter of 1854–55.

In the first parallel the ground is shallow and less cover obtained, but as you approach the place the works are of much larger dimensions. Very thick ramparts and very deep trenches. Generally from the slope of the ground they are pretty well drained, and where there is not sufficient slope, causeways of stones or fascines are made; then the men have burrowed little caves all along the trench.

To the British army of 1855, trained in the tactics of Waterloo, this was a very alien environment but one to which the men soon adapted. The high command, however, did not adapt so well and was unaware of the long term effects of such conditions on the fighting abilities of infantry.

Trench duty normally lasted twelve hours and, despite the issue of warm clothing, there was little that could be done to relieve the miserable conditions which the troops had to endure. In a letter home, Rowlands described his 'kit' for this duty:

My rig now, when for picket, consists of two or three pairs of socks, one over the other. A thick pilot cloth pair of trousers with a piece of red tape down to convert them into regimentals. A thick, warm jersey issued to us by the government, a flannel shirt over that. An ordinary mufti waistcoat and an ordinary pair of boots, into which I thrust foot, three pairs of socks, thick trousers and all.

The position of the 41st placed their trenches well within the range of Russian rifle fire:

I told you in one of my last letters of the French having taken over the Heights of Inkerman. The day they relieved us I was on the left advance, and an officer of the 55th on the right. When they arrived to relieve him, he cautioned them about exposing themselves to the Russian sharpshooters, at which they laughed, and a lot of them jumped up on the parapet for what they call a Cherokee Dance. These were Zouaves, and they had not danced long before four of them were knocked over, which caused them to retreat as sharp as they had got up.

In March, the Grenadier Company moved from its camp at Inkerman into new wooden hutments which had been constructed nearer the trenches. The officers however, remained under canvas as there were insufficient huts to accommodate the entire regiment. Rowlands is on record as being the occupant of a rather novel tent which he shared with his friend, William Allan. They had dug a hole over six feet deep which they then boarded it over with planks looted from a nearby Russian house. The tent was pitched over the whole 'construction', thereby creating an upper and a lower floor to the accommodation. On the lower floor, they had built a small fireplace over which a stove was positioned and, as winter gave way to spring and the weather improved, they found themselves quite comfortable in their somewhat unusual abode.[5]

As the weather changed so did the circumstances of the troops and the parcels which had been longed for during the arduous winter began to arrive. Sent by families and well-wishers back in Britain these contained improved clothing paid for by the public following an outcry after the press had published articles describing the conditions of the army in the Crimea. Rowlands wrote to his mother acknowledging receipt of such a parcel:

I wish you would write to Mrs —, as I don't know her address, and thank her most kindly for her handsome contributions of warm clothing which I received and distributed amongst the men of my company.

The regiment was now employed in extending the trench system to link up with the French on their right. The normal procedure was for half the men to carry out the digging while the other half provided protection. The work was completed, without any major problems, just in the nick of time. On 22 March, 5,000 Russians launched an abortive assault on the French positions with smaller groups attacking the British. The winter of inactivity was over and trench duties became more dangerous as both sides tried to harass the enemy by means of constant raids and sorties against his advanced positions. During the winter months, there had been an unofficial cease-fire during the hours of darkness, but this now came to an end and regiments began to lose a few of their number each night. The absence of any form of censorship enabled Rowlands to described the activities of his company in some detail:

> On Sunday evening I went into the trenches. The weather, which had been threatening for the previous day or two, burst about eight o'clock in the evening, and lasted, without interruption, until eight on the following evening, when we were relieved. I never saw men suffer more; I know I never did. There we were paddling about in mud, averaging from three to eighteen inches in depth. It was worse for us because we were in a new portion of the trench, made the previous day, within fifty yards of the Russians, who had established rifle pits in front of us. They are good marksmen and appear to be always on the lookout, for directly a particle of a body exposes itself, either through a hole in the gabions or over the parapets, so certain would a bullet lodge either in the object aimed at or somewhere near. I was so glad when morning dawned, for I had scarcely a flintlock out of two hundred and fifteen that would go off, so thoroughly were we drenched. If the enemy had come on, we should have been obliged to have depended entirely on our bayonets — no bad things when properly used.

Between 9 and 19 April, the Allied artillery continually bombarded the Russian positions causing immense damage to both their troops and defences. Anticipating that this was the overture before the Allies launched an assault, the Russian commanders decided to maintain high numbers of men in their forward positions as a consequence of which, their losses were very severe — estimated by some to have been as high as 6,000 killed and wounded. As part of their forward defences, the Russians had constructed rifle pits which were a continual source of annoyance to the British advanced trenches. In mid-April, Rowlands was one of the officers involved in an assault upon and capture of these rifle pits and, for the next few days, the men of the 41st were engaged in linking these positions to the existing British trench system.

On 7 June, Lieutenant General Pennefather informed Lieutenant Colonel Eman that the 41st had been selected to attack an enemy position known as the Quarries, which lay to the right of the Woronzoff Road and directly in front of the Redan. The importance of this position was obvious as it formed the last obstacle before an assault could be mounted on the final defensive line of the city of Sebastopol. The regiment's involvement had to be cancelled at the last minute however, as it was deemed that too many of its men were absent on other duties and the task was given to the 49th Regiment who managed to execute the attack successfully. Rowlands expressed his disappointment at being left out of the assault.

Our batteries opened suddenly yesterday (6 June) at 3 o'clock and all day today. The Mamelon [RUSSIAN DEFENSIVE POSITION] is completely silenced, and we have just received intelligence that we are to attack the quarries in front of our advanced work and the French are to take the Mamelon at the same time, it may end in our going beyond our present positions and I trust it may, I hate half measures.

June 9th. We were successful yesterday in taking the quarries and the French the Mamelon. Both sides lost considerably, particularly the French. The quarries were attacked by 200 of the 49th supported by 300 and 47 of our division and a like number of the Light Division. The general sent for our Colonel and told him he was to furnish the attacking party for the quarries but unfortunately, we could not muster the number required, most of our fellows being in the trenches. I wish we had been able for the taking was much easier than the holding of them when taken. I was about from six o'clock in the morning until 8 last night. It was fearfully hot, they showered us with grape and round shot. I had on 74 of the 41st with me and I'm happy to say was very fortunate. I had only one killed and three wounded. You cannot form any idea of the sight displayed along our trenches after capturing the quarries which contained a great number of dead, brains scattered about, hands and legs, thin and headless trunks. I saw one of the 77th smashed to pieces by a 32 pounder. He was struck about the centre of the body and the contents dashed all over us. I hope that ere long we'll be in Sebastopol.

The large working party which had been ordered to hold the Quarries was under Rowlands' command and his actions earned him a Mention in Lord Raglan's despatches. They had to reverse the Russian positions, which had originally been constructed to repel a British attack, so that they could be used to repel any assault from the Russians. The original defensive side of the position had therefore to be removed and the former rear wall built up as the new defensive line. In a letter home, Allan described Rowlands' return:

Rowlands and Peddie [Lieutenant in Nᵒ 6 Company, 41st Regiment] have just returned from the trenches in a dreadful state of filth and dirt, having been relieved … they say it is the worst twenty-four hours they have ever spent, the Russians were very wroth [sic] and kept pounding the trenches and working parties.

Despite the horrors of war, there were some simple pleasures to be found by the officers in the British camp during the late spring and early summer of 1855 and hobbies and interests, although not abundant, did exist. Most of the officers had bought, or in some way acquired, ponies for their own personal use and Rowlands was no exception. As a consequence of this, a regular and very popular event was horse racing which ranged in style from highly organised steeplechases over properly constructed courses, to highly disorganised pony races. Competitions were, on the whole, inter-regimental but 'international' events were held between representatives of each of the Allied armies. Rowlands was particularly fond of these meetings although there is no evidence to suggest that he actually participated in any of the races. Whilst attending, he would meet friends from other regiments and catch up with the social gossip from both the Crimea and their families back in Britain. One particular group of friends included the Hume brothers, John and Robert, who were in the 55th Regiment and Walter and Gustavus, who were in the 38th Regiment. Their friendship was to last a lifetime and it was the son of Robert Hume that was later to marry Rowlands' only daughter.[10] Officers also spent much of their free time visiting or dining with friends either in their quarters or in local establishments such as the *Café de Luxembourg* at Kameish. Another favourite rendezvous was the Inkerman Theatre where amateur dramatic productions were put on for the entertainment of the forces. Officers also went on tours of the Crimean peninsula, often wandering out of the area which was under Allied military control. One such expedition was described by Lieutenant Kingscote of the 41st:

> June 13th, 1855. Started at 2.30 in the morning with Graham, Rowlands and Allan to Baidar. Went out with the French cavalry and *Chasseurs a Pied* to reconnoiter the road to Yalta. Went along the winding road along the cliffs, a most charming view of the sea and the scenery was very pretty. Went about 7 miles without seeing the enemy and took our meal about ¹/₂ a mile this side of Baidar. Got home about 9*pm* having had a very pleasant day. Temperature 96 degrees.

William Allan gave further details of the same expedition:

> We stopped at a house belonging to a Russian nobleman, and being very thirsty we were grateful for some Crimean wine which the caretaker was good enough to give us. On another day Rowlands, Bligh and I went on a jolly picnic near the monastery, chiefly composed of officers of the 2nd Division; the canteen men of the 30th provided the grub; we also had some cricket.

This monastery was that of St. George, situated on the cliffs between Sebastopol and Balaclava. Throughout the war it remained occupied by the monks who conducted regular services. In the words of Captain Hume, 'We spent many happy days at the monastery; it was such a peaceful contrast to our every-day life at the front, within sight and sound of siege and siege guns'.[13]

Distractions aside, the purpose of the Allied presence in the Crimea was the capture of the city of Sebastopol, and that could not be effected without first capturing the final Russian defensive line which hinged upon two features, the Malakov and the Redan. On 17 June, the 41st was ordered to hold itself in readiness to form part of a storming party which was to attack the Redan. At 1*a.m.* the following morning, the regiment made its way down through the network of trenches to take up a position from where it would lead the 2nd Division assault later that day. Only some 500 yards from the Redan, they lay down in the trenches, with strict orders not to show themselves above the parapet. From the start, the attack went badly and the first waves of British troops failed to reach their objectives and began to fall back. Seeing men of the Light Division returning to their trenches, Rowlands leapt out from his position of comparative safety and ran forward into a hail of fire in an attempt to rally the retreating troops and turn them back into the attack. His endeavours however were to no avail, and he was forced to abandon the attempt and return, miraculously unscathed, to his position. At 8*a.m.*, the men of the 2nd Division were ordered to withdraw as the attack had been abandoned and, whilst carrying out this directive, Lieutenant Colonel Goodwyn was slightly wounded, one private was killed and one sergeant and eight further privates were wounded.

Chapter 7
The Redan

The remainder of July and the whole of August was spent in the construction of further trenches as the British line was pushed closer to the Russian defences in preparation for another assault in the near future. The Allied commanders were determined to capture the city before another winter halted their activities and trapped them for a second time. The Russians were equally determined to repel any such attack and, after their success on 18 June, felt confident in their ability to do so. A great conflict was approaching which both sides hoped would finally decide the issue in their favour.

Intelligence reports collected by the Allies from observation and the interrogation of prisoners, suggested that the Russians relieved their garrisons in the trenches and in the Redan each day at noon. In order to reduce the chances of heavy casualties during the changeover, the old garrison was moved out before the new one moved in. It was therefore decided that the assault should take place at this time so as to strike at the enemy when he was at his weakest and potentially most disorganised. The date set for the assault was 8 September.

Three days before the attack, the Allied artillery commenced a bombardment of the Russian defences and the infantry in the advanced trenches kept up a steady rate of fire in order to prevent any effective repairs being carried out. On the night of 5 September, Rowlands, accompanied by twenty men, launched an attack on the Russian rifle pits which they succeeded in capturing. The enemy then counter-attacked and the small force at his disposal proved insufficient to enable the 41st to retain the position and he was forced to order a withdrawal. For his gallantry on this occasion, Rowlands received another Mention in Dispatches.

The bombardment continued throughout 6 and 7 September and observers reported that the Malakov defences had been severely damaged; the abattis, which had seriously delayed the French on the 18

June, had been destroyed in many places. The Redan had also received some damage but nowhere approaching that sustained by the Malakov. It was noted that the French had prepared for their attack with almost scientific precision; nothing had been left to chance, unlike the British General Staff who, once again, was placing too much reliance on the ability of individual soldiers to redeem any shortcomings or unforeseen circumstances which might arise during the battle.

When the regimental officers received their orders on 7 September, many shook their heads in disbelief and predicted another disastrous attack with much the same outcome as that of 18 June. The senior planners appeared to have made every conceivable error and the chances of success were, at the very best, slim. Two divisions were to take part in the assault; the same two that had been involved in the previous abortive effort. By the toss of a coin, the Light Division had again been selected to lead the attack with the first wave made up of elements from the 2nd Battalion of The Rifle Brigade and the 97th Regiment. The second wave, made up of more men from the 97th, accompanied by a detachment from the 90th Regiment, would follow shortly afterwards. These would in turn be followed by working parties made up of 200 men from both divisions and, thirty minutes later, 750 men from the 19th and 88th Regiments, with part of a brigade from the 2nd Division, would act as a support group. The 1st Brigade of the Light Division would act as reserves. The total British assaulting force numbered less than 3,000 men. The French, who were to attack the Malakov, were to lead the assault at noon and only when they had achieved their objective would the British troops leave their trenches and try to storm the Redan.

These arrangements were defective on several grounds.

1. The French assault on the Malakov would warn the Russians that an attack on the Redan was imminent and they would prepare accordingly.
2. If the French succeeded in capturing the Malakov, the Russians would be able to devote their full resources to defending the Redan.
3. The delayed British start would lose them the advantage of the confusion caused by the changeover of the Russian garrison.
4. The use of the Light Division in particular, and also probably the 2nd Division, was a grave error as many of the men had already experienced the formidable defences of the Redan and, significantly, tasted defeat in June. They would, at the very least, be wary of advancing into what many felt was

certain death. Had fresh troops been utilised from some of the other divisions, there would have been an element of ignorance amongst them of what lay ahead and, even those who had a notion of what to expect might see it as an opportunity to show their superiority over the men of the Light Division. It was even rumoured that the 97th Regiment, elements of which were forming the spearhead of the first wave, had only been given this task as a punishment for their failure to obey orders during a minor skirmish some days earlier when they had abandoned their officers under fire.

Whatever misgivings the officers and men may have had, it was too late to change the plans for the assault and, during the evening of 7 September, those men who were to make up the first storming party, made their way into the advanced trenches. At 8*a.m.* on the following morning, Rowlands was amongst those members of the 41st who moved into the extreme right of the Quarries, in the 5th Parallel, just over 200 yards from the Redan where they settled down to wait. Everything now depended on the French.

At noon, the Allied bombardment suddenly ceased and, with a blast of trumpets and a roll of drums, the French infantry swarmed out of their trenches.

Thirty thousand brave men awaited the signal of assault with almost breathless impatience. For months they had longed for that trying hour of danger and glory; they had suffered the long weary hours of trench labour, and the still more weary hours of dull, comfortless inaction, in the hope of planting the tricolour on the battered summit of the fortress, whose adamantine walls and masterly defences had so long baffled all the skill of their engineers and the bravery of their troops.

The Malakov sector (or N° 4 Sector as it was known to the Russians) was defended by some 1,400 infantry drawn from three regiments, 500 artillerymen and some 1,000 sappers and labourers with sizeable reserves bringing the strength up to about 4,000 men.* The Redan sector (or N° 3 Bastion) was positioned in the centre of the line and was defended by some 7,500 men. Inside the Redan itself were two battalions with a reserve battalion on call nearby, probably about 1,500 men. Despite warnings that Allied troops had been spotted moving forward during the morning, dressed, in the case of the French, in full field

* *This contradicts many sources which state that only 1,400 were positioned in the Malakov and is taken from* The Crimean War — A Russian Chronicle, *Albert Seaton, pp210-1*

service order, no action was taken to prepare for an attack. The Russian commanders were convinced that there was no danger and that any assault would come at either dawn or dusk. Consequently, the Russians carried out their normal procedures of changing garrisons at noon and as the time for the attack drew near, many of their soldiers settled down for their lunch, leaving only skeleton gun crews and a few riflemen in position on the parapets facing the Allied army. Even the commander of the Malakov, Major General Bussau, had absented himself and was preparing to decorate a number of men with the Cross of St. George after the lunch break was over.

The French had only 25–40 yards of open ground to cover and reached the Russian positions without a shot being fired against them. The defenders were taken completely by surprise and made hardly any effort to resist; only six of the Malakov's guns managed to fire one round each and within minutes the Malakov was in French hands and the Tricolour had been hoisted. British troops, watching to see the outcome of the events to their right, spotted the flag and stormed out of their trenches and began to run across the 300 yards of open ground in front of them. Despite orders that bayonets were not to be fixed until they crossed the ditches in front of the Redan, most of the troops had fixed them whilst waiting in the trenches. As soon as the men of the Light Division left cover, they were met by a hail of fire from the Russians and everywhere heavy casualties were sustained before they reached the Russian defences. Then came the turn of the 2nd Division.

The first to go over the top were the men of the Grenadier Company of the 41st led by Hugh Rowlands. They rushed to a position to the right of the Light Division but the plans were already going awry. Ahead of them, and directly in their path, was a ditch which had to be crossed by means of ladders, but their progress was blocked by men of the Light Division who had been halted by the severity of the Russian fire and who were desperately seeking cover. Rowlands managed to get his men to push their way through and to cross the ditch but, in doing so, they lost momentum and cohesion and many began to emulate the others around them in seeking cover. On reaching the other side of the ditch, Rowlands led the remainder of the force through a burning opening in the front wall of the Redan and found himself inside where he discovered that they were almost alone as hardly any men of the Light Division had made it that far.

The first British soldier to enter the Redan that day was probably Sergeant Andrew Moynihan of the 90th Light Infantry, who later recalled his feelings as he reached the top of the wall:

> To stay here was certain death; to retreat was not the soldier's way; so I jumped down into the Redan, a distance of about four yards, into the midst of the enemy.

All who tried to follow him were either killed or wounded by the murderous fire from the Russian defenders and, for a few moments he was alone. He was then joined by a private of the 90th and, shortly afterwards, by Lieutenant Graham of the 41st. Together, these three charged the Russian trenches but to no avail and only Moynihan survived. He was then joined by another six or seven men of various regiments commanded by Rowlands. They took up a position in the centre of the Redan, clear of all breastworks and traverses, which they managed to hold for over five minutes before being forced to seek cover behind one of the inner breastworks. If another regiment were to have entered the Redan, Rowlands and his men were convinced that they could have taken the position but, with so few men, there was little that they could do. They were joined by Lieutenant Colonel Maud and six men of the Buffs (3rd Regiment of Foot) and together managed to hold their ground for a further fifteen minutes. Another officer, Lieutenant Swift of the 90th (Light Infantry), was badly wounded and in danger of being killed by a Russian soldier, when Moynihan rushed forward and killed the assailant, but was then himself bayoneted and taken prisoner by two Russians. Rowlands led a small force to his rescue and succeeded in recovering the gallant sergeant.[3]

The struggle was becoming more desperate by the minute and there appeared to be no sign of any reinforcements but, at the same time, fresh Russian troops could be seen moving into the positions ahead of the small band of British soldiers still inside the Redan. By this time, both sides were beginning to run low on ammunition and resorted to throwing any 'missiles' which they were able to get their hands on. Rowlands was struck in the eye and knocked to the ground by some grapeshot thrown by a Russian. No sooner was he back on his feet than he was hit by a similar missile in the other eye and again fell to the ground. Such divine luck could not last much longer.

Outside the Redan, the assaulting troops were beginning to obey their instincts rather than their orders and took cover behind anything that was available. Junior officers did their best to try and get the men to advance into the Redan to relieve those already there, but to no avail. Rowlands tried to get his small command to charge the Russian trench but his men, accustomed to months of comparative safety in the trenches, were unwilling to expose themselves to the enemy's fire. They no doubt realised the futility of such an attempt and knew that not everyone led the charmed life of the young captain who was yelling at them.

Colonel Charles Windham, who was in overall command of the assaulting force, had seen what had occurred and sent several messages back to the British lines urgently requesting reinforcements but to no avail. In the end, he decided that desperate situations called for desperate measures and went back himself to beg for support. By the time he had managed to struggle through to General Codrington who agreed to give him the Royals as reinforcements, it was too late; everywhere, individuals and small groups of men were giving up and beginning to withdraw. Ensign Boscawen Griffith of the 23rd Regiment

A contemporary artist's impression of Colonel Wyndham (centre) and Captain Hugh Rowlands (left) during the second assault on the Redan.

The second assault on the Redan.

(Royal Welch Fusiliers), thought that it was the lack of ammunition which had proved to be the last straw:

> ... a general panic seized our men and they rushed suddenly out of the ditch and back across the open towards our lines, although the officers remained as long as they could and tried to rally the men in every possible way, but it was of no avail.

Major George Ranken, Royal Engineers, felt that it was the loss of gallant men that was the cause of the withdrawal:

> I heard ... that three officers of the 41st, after vainly striving to induce the men to advance, rushed forward together and were all three shot down like one man by the cross-fire of the Russians. This was the turning point ... of the men's indecision —they wavered and fled.

Captain John Hume, 55th Foot, recorded his part in the attack:

> On arriving at the Redan I found the salient angle crowded with men of various regiments, the stormers who had been driven back. Some had penetrated the Redan, but the fire from the flanks of the work was too much for them, broken up as they were by having to cross the 250 yards under a very heavy fire. Some had stopped short under cover instead of rushing the work, and they impeded those who came after them. I found it quite impossible to get my men through the crowd on the salient in any kind of formation, so the only thing to be done was to get through as best we could ... and whatever formation we had was quite destroyed ... If reinforcements had been sent out in proper numbers when we were holding the salient angle I firmly believe that the Redan would have been taken. Shortly after I recrossed the ditch a portion of the earth of the salient angle collapsed with the men that were on it, and then all who were able began to retire, but not before two-thirds of the attacking forces were killed and wounded, upwards of 2,000 out of 3,000 —a large proportion. The Russians ... threw everything they could lay hands on after us, and shot down a great number before we could reach our trenches. A musket-ball smashed my left arm. On getting over the parapet into our lines I met Colonel Windham, who was about to return with a regiment to reinforce the column at the Redan. I told him that it was of no use going on, as all who could had retired. He did not go.

Inside the Redan, Rowlands and his companions saw the last chances of success slip away as the support troops began to move back. They realised that the attack was over and that to remain inside the enemy position meant certain death and so they too began to withdraw.

Rowlands survived with what was now regarded as his usual good luck. As well as the blows to his face (which later developed into two black eyes) he later discovered that a bullet had entered his forage cap, just behind the grenade emblem, and then gone through his hair and that his clothing was pierced in five places by bullets.[7] Bitterly disappointed at the failure of the attack, he was convinced that his men would have followed him into the Redan had they been able to get over the ditch before being slowed up by the congestion created by the Light Division. He, however, had nothing to reproach himself for as far as his own personal conduct was concerned and Major Goodwyn (who had succeeded to the command of the 41st on the death of Lieutenant Colonel Eman in the assault) wrote to Colonel Windham:

> I am glad to report that the conduct of all the officers of the Regt has been highly satisfactory & exemplary—but more especially that of Captains Rowlands and Every.

William Allan wrote in a letter home:

> Rowlands is a brave fellow, but his beauty is for a time rather spoilt ... he will be certain of a brevet and Skipworth also; they deserve it well.

Rowlands also received a mention in the dispatches of Windham and Lt. General Markham, the former having referred to him as '... a fine and gallant young soldier.'

The failure to capture the Redan was a doubly bitter pill to swallow when all knew that the French had achieved their main objective and no one was more keen to discover the reason for this failure than Rowlands who wrote a report on the matter to Windham:

> I examined a few of the soldiers of the 41st and 62nd Foot [Wiltshire Regiment] who formed a part of the assaulting column on the Redan, and discovered that a general opinion prevailed that the place was mined. There was only one exception, a man of the 41st Regiment (perfectly unknown to me) stated that he thought the men generally had no fear of explosions. Upon being asked the cause of that general clinging to the salient, he replied: 'I consider, Sir, that it was entirely owing to a mixture of Regiments, and that a sufficiently large number of the same Regiment, in officers and men, could not be collected for a simultaneous rush into the place.

The disappointment was somewhat short lived for, shortly before midnight, as the dispirited British troops settled down for the night, great explosions were heard coming from Sebastopol and the sky was lit

The view from the Redan after its evacuation by the Russians,
looking towards the British trenches

up by burning buildings and ships. At about 1*am*, curiosity overcame fear and a group of volunteers carefully made their way towards the Redan to discover what was happening. On their return they reported that, save for the dead and dying, the Redan was empty of Russians. The siege was over and the enemy had retreated to the far side of the harbour. It appeared that, having lost the Malakov, the Russian defences were no longer tenable and the high command had therefore ordered a general withdrawal.

The following morning, the Allied commanders entered the Redan where they discovered a scene of such carnage that they ordered sentries to be posted to prevent any of the troops from entering the area until it had been cleared up. One officer however, did manage to get in and recorded what he saw:

> The abattis had been completely smashed by our shot, and had offered but little opposition to the storming party. The open space inside had been ploughed up and torn by our shells. Gabions and fascines had been cut up into chips by them, and the ground was a rugged surface of stones, shot, shell-

The interior of the Redan after the Russian withdrawal.

splinters, lumps of earth and pieces of wood. There were bomb proof craters as in the Malakov, under the salient angle, under the traverses and other available spots. The works were full of unexploded magazines and suspected mines; gabions were burning at all points ... dead Russians were lying in out-of-the-way corners as yet undiscovered or unnoticed by burying parties ... I must have seen three or four thousand dead today.

The captured area of the city which lay south of the harbour was divided into two administrative areas; one under British control and the other under French control. The British sector, known as the Karabelnaya, was placed under the command of Charles Windham (who had been promoted to the rank of brigadier general). As a reward for his services during the siege and assault, Hugh Rowlands was appointed one of five Town Majors andtogether they were to administer the day-to-day running of the city. In October, Windham resumed command of the 2nd Brigade of the 2nd Division and Rowlands went with him as Brigade Major. On 2 November, William Allan's prophecy came true and Rowlands was promoted to brevet major in recognition of his services throughout the Crimean campaign.

Life in the Crimean winter of 1855–6 was far more comfortable than

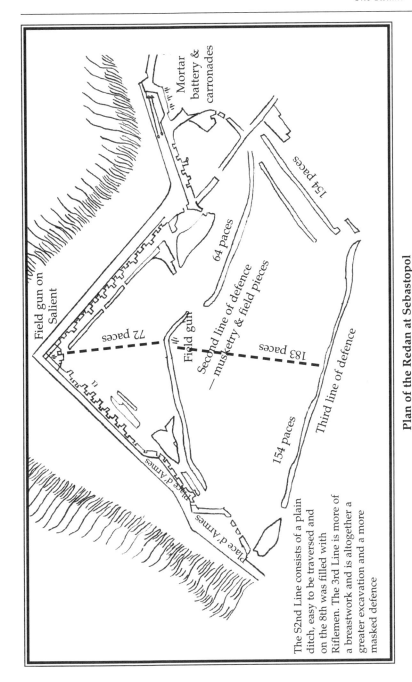

Plan of the Redan at Sebastopol

Based upon an original drawn by Captain Hugh Rowlands, 41st Regiment, on 10 September 1855.
[The original is held in the British Library Maps 148.e.4(22)]

The S2nd Line consists of a plain ditch, easy to be traversed and on the 8th was filled with Riflemen. The 3rd Line is more of a breastwork and is altogether a greater excavation and a more masked defence

Officers and men of the 41st Regiment in the camp at Sebastopol, 1856. On the left is the first goat to become a regimental mascot. Captain Fitzroy is lying on the ground in the centre of the front row. This photograph clearly shows the wooden hutments provided for the army, the variations in the uniforms and the rather dishevelled appearance of the officers at the end of a very unpleasant campaign.

that of the previous year and the days passed without major incident. Winter gave way to spring and, following an armistice, signed at the end of February, peace appeared to be drawing ever closer. Two months later, on 27 April, a peace treaty was signed in Paris and all that remained for the troops in the Crimea was to pack up and prepare for the long journey home. On 17 June, the 41st Regiment marched from its camp to the port of Kameish where it boarded the transport ship *Transit* for the passage home to Britain, via Malta and Gibraltar, finally disembarking at Portsmouth on 28 July.

During this voyage home, Rowlands received news that he had been created a Knight, 5th Class, of the Imperial Order of the Legion of Honour by the French Emperor and a Knight, 5th Class, of the Order of the Medjidie by the Sultan of Turkey. His highest award, granted by his own monarch, was yet to come.

Officers of the 41st Regiment, Sebastopol, 24 May 1856. Standing [L–R]: Assistant Surgeon Gulland, Captain William Allan, Lieutenant Johnson, Colonel Goodwyn, Captain Page, Brevet Major Hugh Rowlands, Quarter Master Elliott, Captain Bligh. Sitting [L–R]: Captain Fitzroy, Major Barnard, Surgeon Scott, Captain Harvey.

The 41st Regiment moved from Portsmouth into barracks at Dover and from there, on 17 August, Brevet Major Rowlands set out for a well earned leave at his north Wales home.

Chapter 8
Hail the Conquering Hero Comes

News of Hugh Rowlands' impending return to Plastirion had preceded him and for some time the local newspaper, *The Carnarvon & Denbigh Herald*, had been reminding people of this fact with headlines like 'The Expected Return of the Gallant and Far-famed Major Rowlands to his Mountain Home'. Not since the return of the 1st Marquis of Anglesey from Waterloo had north-west Wales had a local military hero and the population intended making the most of this opportunity to celebrate. Early in July, a testimonial fund was opened and a committee appointed to decide upon the most suitable manner in which the gallant hero might be recognised. The glory soon began to rub off onto his family who were themselves elevated to the ranks of local celebrities by the press:

> ... a family that will hereafter rank with the noblest of those whose sons have won the laurels of victory and the blazonry of fame.

By the beginning of August, the testimonial fund amounted to over £200 and the committee decided that the money should be used to purchase an ornamental sword and belt to the value of 100 guineas and a dinner service.* It was also agreed that an official civic welcome and address should be made at the railway station upon the arrival of Major Rowlands.

From early morning on 18 August, Caernarfon was a hive of activity as house fronts were decorated, banners and triumphal arches of flowers spanned the streets, shopkeepers decorated their windows with suitably heroic and patriotic displays and people from the surrounding area flocked into the town giving it an air of great festivity. At 4.30*p.m.*, the

---

* *Rowlands declined the offer of the dinner service and asked that the money be given to the families of members of the Grenadier Company who had been killed in the war.*

Mayor, Alderman James Rees,* and the Corporation assembled at the Guildhall and shortly afterwards, began to make their way towards the railway station on Bangor Road; the whole procession being headed by the Llanrug Benefit Society Band. At the station, which was also heavily decorated, a large crowd had been gathering for most of the afternoon (estimated by some to number over 1,000 people) and was already spilling over onto the platform.

At 5.30*p.m.*, as the train carrying Hugh Rowlands came into view, the crowd erupted into loud cheering which continued until he had alighted and the Mayor had called for silence to enable him to make his official speech of welcome. There can be little doubt that Hugh Rowlands was surprised at the reception, but he must have had a foretaste of what to expect from the crowds that had cheered his train through Bangor and the nearby Griffith's Crossing. Throughout his life, he never acquired a reputation as a public speaker but always seemed to know how to appeal to the hearts and minds of his own people around Caernarfon. In reply to the Mayor's welcome, Rowlands said:

> I have not forgotten my country. Indeed, I could not do so for I had the good fortune to belong to a regiment which bears for its title 'The Welsh' and whose motto *Gwell Angau Na Chywilydd* [Better Death than Dishonour] has always been presented to my eye.

This display of patriotism caused the crowd to resume its cheering and, with some difficulty, Rowlands made his way to his carriage in order to begin the final stage of his journey to Plastirion, some four miles distant. All along the route into the town of Caernarfon, the townsfolk lined the pavements cheering enthusiastically and a group of young men stopped the carriage and insisted upon removing the horses in order to draw it themselves, through the streets and along the road leading towards Llanrug. On reaching Pontrug, however, they were met by people from Llanrug who jokingly threatened violence to the 'town boys' if they drew the carriage one step further. No doubt relieved to have their burden removed (the climb from Caernarfon to Pontrug is one of over 200 feet), the Caernarfon men agreed and the journey was resumed. From Bodrual Turnpike the road was again lined with cheering

---

* *The founder of* Y Herald Gymraeg *newspaper and grandfather of Group Captain Lionel W. B. Rees, VC, OBE, MC, AFC of Caernarfon.*

spectators as the villagers vied with each other to welcome home one of their own. Guns placed on the surrounding hills, began to fire a salute which continued until an hour before midnight and, at the parish church, six floral triumphal arches had been erected and the young hero was compelled to make another short speech before proceeding the last half mile home. At 9*p.m.*, three and a half hours after alighting from the train at Caernarfon, Hugh Rowlands crossed the threshold at Plastirion and closed the door upon a day which was '…unparalleled in the annals of Carnarvon' [*sic*] and, as the long summer evening gave way to darkness, bonfires were lit on the surrounding hills which were to burn far into the night.

During the next few days, various events took place to mark Rowlands' safe return, not least of which was the presentation of a gold watch, paid for by voluntary subscription, by the villagers of Llanrug and, on a more informal note, he would have noticed the addition of a number of large, pointed stones in the fields of Plastirion. These had been erected by his father by way of a simple monument to the actions in which his son had been involved during the war. By far and away the most magnificent event however, was that which occurred on Tuesday 9 September when he was instructed to present himself at Caernarfon Castle where he was to receive a presentation and testimonial from the County of Caernarfon.

> The large yard of the castle was completely filled, and every spot about the walls which commanded a view of the proceedings was occupied. A space was ruled off at the bottom area where a platform was erected for discharging the business of the day. A *coup d'oeil* from this elevated position revealed an array of beauty which had scarcely ever before been witnessed within the walls of this ancient fortress, a great proportion being of the fair sex, who invariably show a partiality for military demonstrations … it will not be doubted that their presence in such numbers shed an additional lustre upon the reward decreed by men to be due to the valour of the gallant Major.

At 2*p.m.*, the castle guns opened fire to signal the start of the proceedings and Major Rowlands and the local dignitaries entered the ancient castle to the sound of a choir singing *Hail the Conquering Hero Comes*. Once assembled, the principal members of the committee accompanied by the leaders of local society made their speeches and then presented Rowlands with a richly ornamented Mameluke dress

The Royal Sportsman Hotel, Caernarfon, where a civic dinner was given in honour of Hugh Rowlands on his return from the Crimea.

scimitar (which had been suitably engraved) and a dinner service.* Letters of praise were read out from men who had served with him in the Crimea, before he himself made a short speech of thanks and the proceedings were closed by the Mayor. That evening, a banquet in his honour was held in the coffee room of the Royal Sportsman Hotel which was attended by over one hundred of the local gentry.

After the social whirlwind of his first home leave for nearly three years, it may well have been with some relief that Rowlands returned to his regiment at Shorncliffe on 31 November. In the New Year, the 41st Regiment was ordered to prepare for overseas service in the West Indies and, on 23 January, the Grenadier Company embarked at Portsmouth bound for the island of St. Lucia in the Windward Islands, arriving there sometime in late February. The senior officers of the regiment were stationed on other islands and this therefore became Rowlands' first independent command with three officers, five sergeants, two drummers and one hundred rank and file serving under him.

The island was small, and duties appear to have consisted mainly of keeping down the undergrowth around the barracks. No significant records have survived for this period and one can only assume that the days passed without major incident for the men of the Grenadier Company.

Back in Britain, however, decisions were being taken which were to have a profound effect upon Rowlands' reputation and which would earn him a permanent place amongst the ranks of the brave.

Due to the great courage which had been shown by the army in the Crimea and elsewhere, it had been decided that something should be done by way of recognition. There already existed three methods of rewarding servicemen for distinguished service but each had its limitations. The first, membership of the Order of the Bath, was prohibited to officers below the rank of major and was limited to a fixed number at each level of the order from the highest —G.C.B. — to the lowest — C.B. The second was promotion via a brevet. Again, this was restricted to officers and there was a strong dislike amongst those in positions of authority of pro-moting officers above their seniors in the Army List, believing that to do so would cause resentment. Finally, there was the Mention in Despatches, where an officer, NCO or enlisted man's actions could be drawn to the attention of the Horse Guards and, via the newspapers, the general public. While this was by far the most

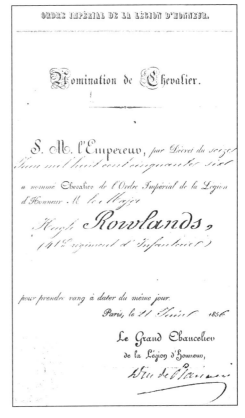

The Order Impérial de la Légion d'Honneur, awarded to Hugh Rowlands by the French Emperor, Napoleon III.

egalitarian of the three rewards, there was no means whereby an individual who had received a Mention in Despatches, could be instantly recognised. In all three cases, however, individuals could be rewarded for valuable service and not just gallantry which meant that the award of a brevet could mean that a man had either been a valuable staff officer or had displayed great courage in action. Following the Battle of Inkerman, Lord Raglan had published his despatches which named *all* the divisional and brigade commanders and *all* their staff officers whether or not they were personally engaged in the fighting.

During the Crimean campaign, the Distinguished Conduct Medal (Army) and the Conspicuous Gallantry Medal (Navy) had been introduced as a means of rewarding the rank and file for courageous actions, but this did not carry with it the prestige of the awards conferred upon British soldiers and sailors by the French and Turkish governments. Indeed, the recognition of the gallantry of certain British servicemen by awarding them the Legion of Honour and the Order of the Medjidie (albeit usually of the lowest class) appears to have caused the authorities considerable embarrassment.

From the first, the discussions about the creation of a new gallantry award were egalitarian in their vision. Captain Scobell, M.P., had said in the House of Commons on 19 December 1854:

> That an humble address be presented to Her Majesty praying that she would be graciously pleased to institute an 'Order of Merit' to be bestowed upon persons serving in the Army or Navy for distinguished and prominent personal gallantry during the present war and to which *every grade and individual, from the highest to the lowest, in the United Services, may be admissible.* [authors italics]

He believed that such a means of recognition would be invaluable for the morale of the men in the Crimea and that the Government and, if necessary, the Crown should look further into the matter.

Almost immediately, with a haste that seems alien to normal governmental activity, the question of such a reward appears to have been taken up by the Duke of Newcastle who wrote to Prince Albert on 20 January.

> I confess it does not seem to me right or politic that such deeds of heroism as this war has produced should go unrewarded by any distinctive mark of honour because they are done by Privates or by Officers below the rank of

Major [a clear allusion to the weakness of the Order of the Bath].

The value attached by soldiers to a little bit of ribbon is such as to render any danger insignificant and any privation light if it can be attained, and I believe that great indeed would be the stimulus and deeply prized the reward of a Cross of Military Merit.

There are some Orders which even Crowned Heads cannot wear, and it would be a military reward of high estimation if this cross could be so bestowed as to be within reach of every private Soldier and yet be coveted by any General at the head of an Army.

Such a reward would have more effect in the Army than the grant of Commissions, and the sight of one of these crosses on the breast of a Soldier returned home invalided would bring more recruits than any of the measures we can now adopt.

Of course, great care would be requisite to prevent abuse, but I am sure Your Royal Highness will not consider the danger of abuse a sufficient reason to reject this proposal if there appears sufficient good in it to justify its adoption.

Newcastle had obviously given the matter considerable thought and within two days received a reply from the Prince stating that he was considering the suggestion and stated:

The only mode I see, in which the difficulty [of rewarding all ranks for acts of gallantry] could be overcome seems to me to be something like the following:

1. That a small cross of Merit for *personal deeds of valour* be established.
2. That it be open to all ranks.
3. That it be unlimited in number.
4. That an annuity (say of £5) be attached to each cross.

Within a week, Newcastle was in a position to announce to the House of Commons that 'Her Majesty has been advised to institute a Cross of Merit which will be open to all ranks of the army in the future'.

Exactly twelve months later, on 29 January 1856, such an award was instituted by Royal Warrant and was named the Victoria Cross. It was to be awarded as a reward for acts of valour carried out by British servicemen (or foreign nationals in the service of the British Crown) in the face of the enemy. The Warrant states that the award was to be granted:

…with a view to place all persons on a perfectly equal footing in relation to eligibility for the order it is hereby declared that neither rank, nor long service, nor wounds, nor any circumstances or conditions whatsoever save the merit of conspicuous bravery shall be held as sufficient qualification for the order.

Report of an Officer ———— recommended for the Order of the Victoria Cross.—

Name.	Act of Valour for which he is recommended
Captain (now Major) Hugh Rowlands 41st Reg.	For rescuing Colonel Mostyn of the 41st Reg. from Russian Soldiers, Col. Mostyn having been wounded and surrounded by them, and for gallant exertions in recovering the ground occupied by his Company's Picket, against the superior numbers of the Enemy, in the ordnance, ... Battle of Inkerman ...

The creation of such an award was met with mixed feelings for, whilst many agreed that such a distinction was well deserved and long overdue, others felt that it was no more than the duty of all servicemen to carry out their tasks with the utmost courage and that to single out certain individuals would be an insult to the other men who took part in the same action. A Royal Warrant, however, made the award a fact and, irrespective of their personal feelings, all commanding officers of regiments and ships were asked to submit the names of any officers, NCOs or men whom they considered might be worthy of the award. These names would then be viewed by the Admiralty and the War Office and, suitably annotated, they would then be passed to Lord Panmure, the Secretary for War, who in turn would pass them on to the Queen for the final selection and approval.

Hugh Rowlands was one of those nominated for the new award by Colonel Haly of the 47th Regiment and the nomination was approved by the Horse Guards, Panmure and the Queen and was published in the *London Gazette* on 24 February 1857, the citation reading:

> For having rescued Colonel Haly of the 47th Regiment, from Russian soldiers, Colonel Haly having been wounded and surrounded by them, and for gallant exertions in holding the ground occupied by his advanced picket against the enemy, at the commencement of the Battle of Inkerman.

It has now become fashionable to play down the early awards of the Victoria Cross by suggesting that many of them were awarded for acts of gallantry which, in later years, would have merited a much lower award, most notably, post-1915, the Military Cross or Military Medal. This opinion undoubtedly stems from the brevity of the original citations and, had these citations been written so as to provide full details of the acts of gallantry, as in the case of modern awards, then a very different view might now be held. It is invidious to try to compare awards made for acts of gallantry in the mid-19th century with those made at later dates, particularly during the two World Wars for who can tell which required the greater courage. Surely it is not the degree of one man's courage that should be measured against that of another at a different time. Instead, all that matters is that, *in the eyes of their contemporaries*, those men

Facing: The citation for the Victoria Cross awarded to Hugh Rowlands for his gallantry at Inkerman, 5 November 1854. [Public Record Office]

Report of an Officer ——————— recommended for the

Order of the Victoria Cross

Name	Act of Valour for which he is recommended

awarded the Victoria Cross were deemed to be worthy of the nation's highest recognition and respect. The Crimean VCs were seen by their peers as men of great individual courage who merited this acknowledgement.

Certainly, in the case of Hugh Rowlands, there would appear to be little question that his award was justified and an interesting feature of the selection of his name for the VC is the fact that he actually received two nominations. In addition to that detailed above, he was also nominated by Lieutenant General Pennefather for his actions during the first assault on the Redan. The wording of this second citation reads:

> Distinguished on a hundred occasions in action and in the trenches. Particularly gallant and devoted in jumping out of the trenches under a terrific fire and rallying soldiers of the Light Division, beaten back by the Russians. Attack on the Redan, 18th June, 1855.

The choice of words in this citation, which was initially accepted by the War Office committee, was unfortunate as they can only be described as vague in the extreme and, had Pennefather taken greater care, then this might have been the citation for which the eventual award was made. The selectors could not, however, make two awards to the same person as the regulations, if strictly interpreted, did not allow for such a circumstance. Clause 4 of the Royal Warrant stated:

> ...that anyone who, *after having received the Cross*, shall again perform an act of bravery which, if he had not received such Cross, would have entitled him to it, such further act shall be recorded by a Bar attached to the ribband by which the Cross is suspended.

As no VCs had been awarded before 1857 there was no Crimean recipient who had already received the decoration and therefore no claims to Bars could be accepted in relation to acts of gallantry performed during that campaign. Another consideration when looking at the two nominations and trying to decide which should merit the award is the circumstances surrounding each. At Inkerman, Rowlands had played a significant role in a military action which, although confused, resulted in a resounding British victory whereas the first

Facing: The second citation for a Victoria Cross for Hugh Rowlands' gallantry during the first assault on the Redan, 1855. [Public Record Office]

assault on the Redan, gallant though it may have been, had proved an abject failure.

One further interesting point with regard to the award to Hugh Rowlands is the fact that no mention is made in either citation of his actions during the second attack on the Redan. There can be no question that his services on that day were regarded by all as having displayed the highest levels of gallantry. The senior officer in command of the assaulting parties, Colonel Windham, made several references to the bravery of Rowlands and was instrumental in obtaining for him the positions of Town Major of Sebastopol and Brigade Major. It was the events of that day which had made the award of his Brevet Majority inevitable and yet, there was no mention of it amongst the VC nominations. Amongst those who, like Rowlands, attacked the Redan on that fateful day, no fewer than nine men received the Victoria Cross, namely, Lieutenant Colonel Maude, Major Charles Lumley, Captain Gronow Davis, Assistant Surgeon Thomas Hale, Assistant Surgeon William Sylvester, Sergeant Andrew Moynihan, Sergeant Daniel Cambridge, Corporal Robert Shields and Private John Connors. Whether the omission of Rowlands from this list was because it was felt that he had already been adequately rewarded for his actions by the promotion to Brevet Major, or whether there was some other unknown reason will never be known but it does make interesting private speculation.

In June 1857, those recipients who were in Britain, were decorated with the Victoria Cross by Queen Victoria in a special ceremony held in Hyde Park. Such a public display of courage undoubtedly played a prominent part in the adoption of the Victoria Cross by the British public, as a symbol of supreme bravery, a status which it still holds today. Indeed, the Victoria Cross holds a special place throughout the world as a reward for outstanding gallantry, unrivalled by any other nation's decoration. The sight of the small brown cross or the letters 'VC' after a recipient's name are sufficient to place him on a pedestal even today when great military events are, in the main, faint memories from the distant past.

Facing: Major Hugh Rowlands, shortly after his return from the Crimea, 1856. This re-touched photograph shows him sporting the newly fashionable 'Imperial' style beard. Taken before he was decorated with the Victoria Cross, this photograph has an inaccurate impression of the award drawn on to his left chest.

Rowlands, being in the West Indies, was unable to attend the ceremony and so his Cross was sent to the senior officer in the Caribbean who was instructed to make the award on behalf of the Queen. On 5 August, Rowlands was decorated with the Victoria Cross by Major General Sir Josias Cloete at Barbados.

After a short leave, Rowlands returned to St. Lucia on 20 August where, about a month later, he was taken seriously ill with a fever. Precise details of this illness have not survived but it may have been yellow fever, a disease peculiar to the tropics and, in particular, the West Indies. It caused severe back pain, fever, acute headaches, a yellow-green colouration of the skin and hallucinations. At the time, the cause of the disease was unknown (it is carried by mosquitos) and the only treatment, if the sufferer was to have any chance of survival, was to remove him from the high temperatures of the tropics. If the patient was lucky, he would recover but it was a slow process. Alternatively, it may have been malaria, also transmitted by mosquitos, which was likely to recur throughout the infected person's life. On 6 November, Rowlands was placed on half-pay which meant that he had to vacate his post and command, which was then given to another officer, and he was retired from active service. At that time, half-pay was the only means available of retaining the potential services of an officer whilst at the same time reducing the costs to the Exchequer. On 13 December, Rowlands was promoted from Captain and Brevet Major to Major which entitled him to a higher rate of half-pay and allowed him to maintain his seniority in the regiment. On the same day, he embarked for home, arriving back in Britain sometime during January 1858, by which time he had recovered sufficiently to travel to north Wales where he remained in the care of his family for several months.

For a man with a reputation for action, this period of forced inactivity must have been difficult to endure and he appears to have made every effort to return to full-pay as quickly as possible and by July, he was attached to Major General Lawreson's Brigade at Aldershot as a Staff Officer. Five weeks later he was serving with the Depôt of the 3rd/7th Regiment (Royal Fusiliers) at Chatham and in January of the following year, he took acting command of the Battalion where he appears to have been a popular officer earning such comments in the regimental records as '...everyone appreciated the kindness shown towards them by that officer.' He remained with the 7th Foot until 26 August when he was again placed on half-pay.

This time, his stay away from duties was longer and may have been the result of a recurrence of the fever, and he did not return to full-pay until early the following year when he rejoined the 41st Regiment which had returned from the West Indies and was stationed in the Isle of Wight, carrying out various engineer duties. The regiment remained on the island until the spring of 1862 when it was ordered to the north of England (Rowlands being stationed at Newcastle upon Tyne) and in March 1863, they moved to Scotland (Rowlands being posted to Glasgow).

Shortly before this last move, in February 1863, Hugh's father, John Rowlands, died at Plastirion, leaving his entire estate to his widow for the remainder of her life. He stipulated, however, that on the death of Elizabeth Rowlands, the estate was to be divided up in the following manner:

1. £3,000 was to be given outright to his daughter Elizabeth.
2. An annuity of £300 was to go to his eldest son John.
3. The residue of the estate after the above provisions had been carried out was to go to Hugh.

As Hugh was the youngest son, this was a somewhat unusual arrangement and local 'legend' had it that John was the black sheep of the family, having married a young lady whose family was in the licenced trade. As far as Hugh was concerned, the importance of the will was that, on the death of his mother, he would have an independent income which he could use to supplement his army pay. This would be a complete turn-around in his prospects and would place him in a position to consider not only promotion to the higher ranks of the service, should such an opportunity arise, but also to consider the possibility of marriage. Previously, the idea of taking a wife would have been ridiculous when he had to rely entirely upon his army pay (or half-pay) as it was quite inadequate for his routine military and living expenses. It would appear that it was at this time that he met the young lady who was to become his wife. Isabella Jane was the daughter of late Thomas Raikes Barrow, RN, of Stroud, Gloucestershire. Her paternal grandfather had been a military man, Lieutenant Colonel Barrow of the Coldstream Guards and her mother was Elizabeth, daughter of William

Glynne Griffiths of Rhosfawr and Bodegroes, near Pwllheli, Caernarfon-shire. The Rowlands' and the Griffiths' had known each other for many years and both families had served as stewards to the Newborough Estate and Hugh had been a close friend of Isabella's uncle, David White Griffith, since childhood.

The suggested logic behind his embarking on a military career, in order to carve a career for himself was now outdated and he could very easily have resigned his commission in order to return to Llanrug to run the family estate on behalf of his mother, secure in the knowledge that on her death it would pass to him. This he did not do and there is no evidence that he had any thought other than to remain in the army where he was poised to move up to the command of a battalion.

In April 1864, the 41st was moved to the Curragh near Dublin where it remained until July of the following year when it embarked for Calcutta, India, arriving there on 5 November. After a month of re-equipping and acclimatisation, the regiment marched to Agra, one of the hottest stations in the sub-continent, where Rowlands, now a Brevet Lieutenant Colonel, assumed command in place of Colonel Goodwyn who had been promoted to command the Benares Brigade in Bengal. On 23 March 1866, at the age of 38, Hugh Rowlands was promoted to Lieutenant Colonel and confirmed in the position of officer commanding the 41st Regiment of Foot.

He had now reached what many regard as the pinnacle of a military career, command of his own regiment, and no other position, no matter how lofty or important, can compare with that of Lieutenant Colonel. The difficult, insecure years when he had been on half-pay were now safely behind him and he was stationed in India where the standard of living for British officers was high whilst the living costs were low; the time had come to settle down. His bride-to-be was twenty-one years his junior but this was not unusual in British society in the mid-19th century when compatibility came a poor second to social standing. In terms of the latter, the marriage would have been regarded as a good match both in Caernarfonshire —where both families had a comparable social

*Facing: Major Hugh Rowlands, c.1859, after his return to the 41st Regiment.
The decorations, medals and service sword shown here are
displayed in the Welch Regiment Museum, Cardiff Castle.*

Above: Lt. Colonel Hugh Rowlands, VC, CB, with the officers of the 41st Regiment at Mooltan, India, 1870.

Below: Lt. Colonel Hugh Rowlands, VC, CB, with the officers of the Welch Regiment at Mooltan, India, 1877. Standing on Rowlands' left is his friend William Allan.

standing— and in the military society of the British army. There was no possibility of the groom returning to Britain for the wedding and so the marriage took place at Serampore on 2 November 1866. In addition to stability and marital status, his young wife brought with her a sizeable financial settlement of £5,000 — plus an additional £11,500 which was to be the subject of a protracted legal battle before it was finally paid.

At this stage it is interesting to study Hugh Rowlands' career from a purely statistical viewpoint. The average age for promotion to the rank of Lieutenant Colonel during the mid-19th century was 49; he attained the rank at the age of 38. He had entered the service at the age of 21, which was the average age for an Ensign at that time but, with the exception of his promotion to Captain, he had advanced through the commissioned ranks purely by merit and it could be argued that, for a man with no military background and little social influence with the Horse Guards, he had had a remarkable career. It augured well for the future and it seemed possible that the highest ranks of the army were coming within his reach.

The days at Agra passed without incident and, towards the end of 1868, the 41st received orders that it was to move to Subathoo early the following year. Isabella was, by this time, pregnant with their first child and, in order to minimise the risks of a journey too close to the date of confinement, she preceded the regiment to its new station where, on 9 January, she gave birth to a daughter who was christened Violet Margaret Isabel. Just over a year later, their second child was born, a son who was christened Hugh Barrow.

In November 1870, the 41st left Subathoo and moved to Mooltan where they relieved the 109th Regiment (The Leinster Regiment). Again, the days passed without incident and little information has survived about Rowlands' activities beyond the day-to-day running of the regiment. Again, he appears to have earned a reputation as a fair and very courteous senior officer as witnessed by a young officer of the Gordon Highlanders, 2nd Lieutenant Ian Hamilton* who, in 1874, arrived at the station expecting to find his own regiment there and who spent several days as a guest of the 41st.

---

* *Later General Sir Ian Hamilton (1853–1947), who commanded the ill-fated operations at Gallipoli during the First World War.*

So soon as I had unpacked some of my things ...and made myself tidy we went over to the Mess and I left cards on the Colonel and Officers of the 41st ...the Secretary forthwith handed me an invitation to consider myself an honorary member of the Mess and asked me to dine that night as a guest. That night was not a regular Guest Night so I sat in great glory on the right hand of the Colonel and was given champagne like a prodigal son. The Colonel was one of the handsomest men I have ever met —rather on the lines of Napoleon III and like him wearing an imperial on his chin.

During the period of his command at Mooltan, Rowlands was promoted to Colonel (23 March 1871) and managed to acquire a reputation as a more than capable military commander. In a letter dated 1869, the Horse Guards notified the Commander-in-Chief, India that 'the great improvement stated to have taken place in the 41st Regiment has been specially noticed with approval by His Royal Highness.' The following year the praise was even more personal when Rowlands received a letter from the office of the Divisional Commander:

> As the 41st is about to leave the Division, I am directed to convey to you the expression of his [Major General Fordyce] sense of the high state of the drill to which you have brought the Corps, and of his satisfaction at the discipline and interior economy shown at the last inspection and the Major General considers the efficiency of the Regiment most creditable to you as Commanding Officer ...the whole set up of the Regiment testifies to your painstaking zeal as well as to your intelligence and aptitude for the position you hold.

In 1874, as a prelude to returning to Britain, the battalion was posted to Aden where it again received a very favourable report on its military bearing and efficiency. On 5 March, it embarked aboard the *Euphrates* and arrived at Portsmouth at the end of the month.

Rowlands' mother had died on 21 January 1875, whilst he was still in the Middle East and, as stipulated in his father's will, the bulk of the Plastirion Estate now passed to him. The effect of this change of circumstances was considerable as, for the first time in his life, he became financially independent. The exclusion of his older brother from the estate (with the exception of his annuity), meant that Rowlands now had the full benefit of the 1,000 plus acres which would provide him with an additional gross income of over £1,000 *per annum*.

On its return to Britain, The Welch Regiment (as the 41st was being called by the mid-1870s) was stationed at Shorncliffe and it was there, on

A hand-coloured portrait photograph of Colonel Hugh Rowlands, VC, CB, in India,
c.1878. There appears to be an error in the rank badges on his collar.
[Museum of Welsh Life, St. Fagans]

12 May 1875, after nearly twenty-six years service, that Rowlands left it to exchange with Lieutenant Colonel Jordan and take command of the 1st Battalion The Border Regiment (34th Foot) which was about to be posted to India. He had acquired a taste for service in the sub-continent and was obliged to relinquish his command of The Welch as a Colonel could only carry out the duties of a field officer in the same regiment for a maximum period of five years from the date of his appointment. This was done in order to ensure a continuation of promotions within regiments which would not have been possible if commanding officers were permitted an unlimited tenure of office. As Lieutenant Colonel Jordan had only just been promoted, the arrival of Rowlands would not affect the other officers prospects of promotion. A return to India offered, in addition to the higher pay and lower living expenses, the attraction of possible service on the north-west frontier. Two weeks after his exchange, Rowlands received his final honour for his services in the Crimea when he was created a Military Companion of the Order of the Bath. Admission to this order of chivalry was restricted and new nominations were obliged to wait for existing members to be either elevated to a higher class or to die in order that vacancies might be filled and, for this reason, awards were often made, as in the case of Rowlands, many years after the period of distinguished service for which they were granted.

On 29 September, the 34th Regiment sailed from Queenstown, Ireland and arrived in Bombay on 31 October from where it was transferred to Ferozopore. Rowlands' reputation as an efficient battalion commander was not without justification and the 34th, which could not be said to have been held in very high regard when it left Britain, soon began to show the effects of the change of command and, less than a year after its departure from Ireland, Rowlands received a report from the Divisional Commander:

> Everything connected with this regiment appears to be in a high state of efficiency and His Royal Highness [The Duke of Cambridge, C-in-C of the British Army] desires that his commendation be conveyed to Colonel Rowlands its Commanding Officer.

That the improvement was not a temporary affair is clearly shown when, two years later, the Adjutant General recorded:

Major General Stewart's report upon the 34th Regiment is most creditable both as regards Colonel Rowlands and this excellent regiment.

By 1877, Rowlands was feeling that his career was stagnating and there seemed to be little hope that the 34th Regiment would see any active service in the foreseeable future. His period in command of the battalion was nearing its end and his inability to speak any of the native languages of India debarred him from being appointed to the Staff. The Duke of Cambridge was aware of the situation and wrote:

> The language is a sad difficulty in the selection of Line Officers for the most important posts. This regulation debars Colonel Rowlands, 34th, and many other good officers.

Rowlands returned to Britain late in the year and arranged a personal interview with the Commander-in-Chief where they discussed his future employment. He requested that he be given the command of the 43rd Regiment (Oxfordshire Light Infantry) but, unfortunately, the vacancy had already been filled. Cambridge wrote to General Sir Paul Haines, the C-in-C India, in January 1878:

> I had no idea that he [Rowlands] wished for this transfer which could so easily have been arranged for him. Now of course it is too late. Could you not give him a Brigade Command in either Presidency?

The problem of future employment was, however, soon solved from a most unexpected quarter when Lieutenant General the Honorable Frederick Augustus Thesiger was appointed to the command of all British forces in Cape Colony. Thesiger had served in the Crimea and in India where he had been acquainted with Rowlands' reputation as a courageous officer and a highly esteemed regimental commanding officer. He decided that Rowlands fitted the requirements for active service against the native tribes in southern Africa and requested his services as an ADC on his staff. The latter quickly accepted the offer and was appointed a Special Service Officer, on half-pay from the British Army. His actual duties were undefined and would very much depend upon the situation on his arrival in the colony.

Chapter 9
Commandant of the Transvaal

The background to the situation in southern Africa was complex as the three-way struggle between the British, the Boers and the native African tribes had been going on for many years. The periodic wars between the white settlers and the black tribes were traditionally grouped together under the generic, but disparaging title of the Kaffir Wars and, when Lieutenant General Thesiger took over the military command of the region from Lieutenant General Sir Arthur Cunynghame, the 9th Kaffir War was being waged against the great chief Sindali. By March however, the conflict appeared to be drawing towards its close and all that remained was the 'mopping-up' operations which were required in order to crush the few remaining pockets of resistance.

The exact date of Rowlands' arrival in South Africa is unrecorded but he was certainly present in Cape Colony by 11 March 1878. With activities being wound down, the allocation of suitable posts for those officers newly arrived in the colony was to prove a difficulty and two officers in particular, Rowlands and Evelyn Wood,VC, were posing a dilemma. The General saw both as being men of action and did not think that they would be satisfied with an administrative position; indeed, both had left such posts in order to serve at the Cape. Thesiger wrote to Sir Bartle Frere, Governor of Cape Colony, regarding the problem:

> As regards the appointment of Inspector of all the Colonial Forces either Colonel Evelyn Wood or Colonel Rowlands would fit it well, but I have some doubts whether either would care to accept it. £1,300 a year is, I understand, the pay which the Colonial Secretary proposed to give and that sum ought to be sufficient to tempt a good officer to come out from England.

Rowlands did accept the post, however, and was given Captain Frederick Carrington, of the 24th Regiment (2nd Warwickshires), to assist him. Carrington had already distinguished himself during the recent operations in the colony and was well known as an organiser of mounted volunteers and it was he who raised the unit, originally called Carrington's Horse, which later became the famed Frontier Light Horse.

Most of the colonial volunteers who were on active service were stationed in the recently annexed territory of the Transvaal and, following Rowlands' appointment, Thesiger wrote to Sir Theophilus Shepstone, the British Administrator in Pretoria:

Captain Frederick Carrington.

> You will find Colonel Rowlands a very reliable officer. I am certain you may trust him and Carrington to organise your volunteers forces, and to give the best possible advice as to their employment.

Rowlands commenced his duties by embarking upon a lengthy tour of all the outposts in the Transvaal. Everywhere he went he appears to have created a favourable impression and at Fort Weeber, Captain Clarke, the British Commissioner, said: 'I liked what I saw of Colonel Rowlands very much' and Shepstone concurred with this view when he wrote 'From the little I have seen of Colonel Rowlands I should judge that he is an able and well qualified officer.'

Not everything that Rowlands saw during his tour of inspection was to his liking. At Utrecht, he criticised the position of the camp, the guards and the drill which the men performed. But, as he pointed out to Shepstone, he was not in a position to do anything other than comment — 'My position is such that I cannot interfere with any Military arrangement, which I regret, for I know that I might have been of some use.'[7] This frustration at his inablility to control the situation, for which he might be deemed to be responsible, was a factor which was to recur throughout his period of command in South Africa. As he travelled around the Transvaal he became captivated by the barren, rugged countryside and expressed a desire to remain in the region in any suitable capacity. In June, he visited the capital, Pretoria, and inspected the forces that were gathered there, amongst whom were volunteers from Natal* and he was far from satisfied with what he found:

> The horses provided for the men were such as would not be worth £3 on the Kimberley market. Most of them were unable to proceed, and the remainder were a most miserable lot of weeds.

The commander of the volunteers, Captain Stewart, had applied for a Board to be set up which could examine the horses but his request had been turned down '… the authorities knowing that every horse of about 130 would be condemned'.[9] Rowlands agreed with the Captain's assessment of his mounts and told him that he would be perfectly justified in refusing to take a single one. Stewart in fact selected forty and rejected the remainder, an action which incensed Shepstone, who then refused to confirm Stewart's commission and ordered the Natal Mounted Volunteers to proceed without him, under the direct command of Colonel Owen Lanyon, a regular British officer. Without exception, the force supported the Captain and refused to serve under any other officer. The local press picked up the story and, by the end of the month, it was published in *The Times of Natal*, causing considerable embarrassment to Shepstone and all the officials concerned.

At the same time as the row over the Natal Mounted Volunteers broke out in the press, Rowlands again found himself in conflict with the Transvaal authorities as, after completing his inspection at Pretoria, he travelled to Middelburg where he uncovered another scandal which was also quickly picked up by the newspapers. He discovered four wounded men, who had been sent down from the front line, housed in one small room with only one thin blanket each and nothing else except the bare walls. They had no beds or furniture of any description in the 'hospital' and the orderly in charge told Rowlands that the government would not give him the authority to buy anything. Rowlands ordered him to buy whatever he required in order to take proper care of the wounded and that he would accept the responsibility. *The Times of Natal* reported:

---

* *When Sir Theophilus Shepstone had annexed the Transvaal he had gathered together a forces of irregulars to supplement the 1/13th Light Infantry who were garrisoning Pretoria. Among these units were the Lydenburg Volunteer Corps, Raaff's Transvaal Rangers, the Diamond Fields Horse and the Zulu Police.*

… had it not been for him [ROWLANDS] the men who had come up as volunteers, fighting for the Transvaal government, been wounded, that Government would have allowed them to lie there and die, for all they cared, not only without medical assistance, but even without proper food and bedding.

There can be little doubt that these two incidents did little to endear Rowlands to the authorities in the Transvaal and to Shepstone in particular but, such was Rowlands' personality that such upsets were quickly forgotten during the difficult times that lay ahead. His willingness to rock the administrative boat over such incidents shows the concern that he always had for those under his command, irrespective of the consequences to himself. This attitude had been in evidence throughout the Crimean campaign and during his peacetime service since 1856. He believed that a man should be turned into as good a soldier as possible and that it was the responsibility of those in authority over that soldier to do everything in their power to ensure that he was as well cared for as the situation would allow. He did not believe in discomfort for its own sake and was certainly opposed to any unnecessary injury or loss of life. This attitude, although so obviously sensible in our eyes today, was to lead to serious repercussions for Rowlands before the end of the year.

Chief Sindali, the main source of opposition to British rule in southern Africa, died in June 1878, and, following an amnesty proclaimed on 29 June, the hostilities with the Ngqika were over. This, however, did not bring peace to the colony as in Griqualand West and in the two districts of the Transvaal (one near Bloemhoff and the other near Lydenburg, in an area known as Sekhukhune's Country) hostilities continued unabated.

After Cetshwayo, the king of the Zulus, Sekhukhune, the chief of the Pedi, was generally regarded as the most powerful of the Basuto chieftains. The Pedi recognised the supremacy of the Zulu and Cetshwayo was referred to as the 'Bull' whilst Sekhukhune was the 'Calf'. The latter's tribal area was in the Lulu mountains of the north-eastern Transvaal and consisted of a wilderness of sand, rock and thorn bush. His capital, known as Sekhukhune Town, was situated in the midst of these mountains and was believed to be impregnable.

In 1876, the then independent Boer government of the Transvaal Republic had attempted to take possession of the area known as the

Chief Sekhukhune of the Pedi, photographed after his capture in 1879.

Disputed Territories on the bank of the Blood river, which the Zulu king, Cetshwayo, claimed belonged to his people. As a consequence of this dispute, Sekhukhune took up arms against the Boers on behalf of his overlord. The Boers, assisted by Swazis (who were renowned for their savagery and were the traditional enemies of both the Zulu and the Pedi), invaded Sekhukhune's territory where amid the rocks and thorn bushes they were lured into ambush after ambush. Disillusioned with their lack of headway the Boer volunteers began to hold back before drifting back to their homes. The Swazis did make some headway against the truculent chief but, when they saw their allies departing with the cattle that their warriors had captured, they also withdrew in disgust. The assaulting forces returned to the Transvaal with severe losses and no further attempts were made to subdue the truculent Pedi who resumed their raids on the border area. At that time, the British did not regard Sekhukhune as a rebel and declared that as his territory had never been a part of the Transvaal, the action of the Boers was an unjustified act of aggression against an independent ruler. In April 1877, the situation had changed dramatically when the British annexed the Boer Republic of the Transvaal and with it, the Boer claims to Sekhukhune's country. But, for a time, relations between the chief and his new neighbours remained reasonably cordial.

According to the treaty which had 'ended' the war between the Boers and the Pedi, the latter had agreed to pay 2,000 head of cattle as compensation to the government in Pretoria. The annexation of the Transvaal and Britain's attitude towards the whole affair resulted in the terms of this agreement not being fulfiled and Sir Theophilus Shepstone, as British Administrator in Pretoria, adopted a new position by siding with the Boers and instructing Sekhukhune to comply with the terms of the treaty. He chose the wrong time to make his demands as there had been a severe drought in the region which had played havoc with the native cattle and the thought of surrendering 2,000 head to the British was unthinkable to a society which based its social system upon the ownership of cattle. Sekhukhune, by way of a gesture to the British, handed over 200 emaciated animals. Shepstone refused to accept this reduced payment and demanded the numbers as specified in the agreement at which point Sekhukhune decided to take matters into his own hands and, in February 1878, he ordered a force of his warriors, along with those of his sister Legolwana, to attack a neighbouring chief, named Pokwana, who was friendly to the British, and under the protection of the troops stationed at Fort Weeber. After a short, but fierce struggle, the Pedi were repulsed but the twenty-five men at Fort Weeber had been forced by lack of numbers to stand by without taking any action against the aggressors. This passivity encouraged Sekhukhune who then turned his warriors on the white settlements which were encroaching into what he claimed was his territory, an offensive which resulted in the death of one farmer. Captain Clarke the British officer commanding at Fort Weeber sent a message to the chief expressing the strong objection of the British government to the recent events to which Sekhukhune replied by stating that the British were afraid of him, that they were trespassing on his land and demanded that they leave immediately. He added that he was ready to use further force against any British troops that might be sent into his territory. Such defiance was seen as blatant provocation by the British authorities but they were in no position to take any action against the Pedi as the three companies of the 1/13th Regiment (Somersetshire Light Infantry) that were stationed at Pretoria, could not be moved as there was a general fear that the Boers were awaiting just such an opportunity to rebel against the annexation of the Transvaal. A request was therefore made that more troops be despatched to Pretoria from the force at Thesiger's disposal in Natal. The British Administrator also appealed to the Boers who were resident in the Transvaal, asking them to volunteer for service against Sekhukhune, but they had already experienced the problems of fighting in Sekhukhune's country and did not wish a repetition of the events of the previous year. Above all, however, the Boers saw no reason why they should assist the British in any manner as they regarded the 'redcoats' as being just as much their enemy as were the Pedi warriors.

Thesiger was now in a dilemma. He could not spare any more troops for the Transvaal but neither did he want a full-scale native uprising in the area. Before reaching any decision about the appropriate action, he received news that Shepstone, by his persistence, had eventually managed to raise a small force of fifty volunteers in Pretoria which were quickly ordered to Fort Weeber to reinforce Clarke's small garrison. On 5 April, the volunteers, accompanied by friendly natives, attacked Masselaroom, Legolwana's stronghold but the town was strongly defended and the volunteers were forced to withdraw after only modest success. Thesiger felt that Shepstone's actions were unlikely to impress the native chief and that some decisive action should be taken at once and, consequently, on 16 April, two companies of the 1/13th were ordered out of Pretoria to march to Lydenburg and the remaining company of the 1/13th was sent to Middelburg. The threat presented by these reinforcements led to the surrender of Legolwana's tribe, without further incident, at the end of April.

Sir Theophilus Shepstone.

This minor British success did not deter Sekhukhune who continued with his acts of aggression and his threats. The British troops remained inactive during May whilst the Pedi attacked isolated farms and, on 3 July, probably disgusted by the lack of any action on the part of their professional allies, the local volunteers attacked the Magnet Heights in the southern part of the Lulu mountains. They were driven back with sixteen casualties, including seven dead. A little over three weeks later, another volunteer was killed and some horses captured during one of the Pedi raids and, on 7 August, Sekhukhune's warriors took fifty-two horses and forty-eight oxen belonging to the Diamond Fields Horse. Such unrest, with no real retaliation on the part of the British authorities, led to a mutiny amongst the local native police who had to be quickly disarmed.

As the situation continued to deteriorate, it became obvious that the government would have to take some form of military action against the troublesome chief as, if they did not, the revolt might well spread to other, potentially more dangerous tribes, in particular the Zulu. Early in July, Thesiger had appointed Rowlands to the position of Commandant of the Transvaal with instructions to destroy the ever present threat from Sekhukhune's Country. The General wrote to Shepstone:

Sir Bartle seems to consider it was important that Your Excellency should have an officer at your right hand who could act at once, on his own responsibility and who would report direct to me.

This letter is somewhat ambiguous in that it implies that Rowlands' new command was to be independent whilst at the same time under the control of both Shepstone and Thesiger, who would be several hundred miles away, unaware of the circumstances in the Transvaal and, as such, in no position to directly influence events. Perhaps surprisingly, considering Rowlands' earlier criticism of the Transvaal authorities, Shepstone was pleased with the appointment:

> I was glad to find you had decided upon the appointment of Colonel Rowlands as Commandant of the Transvaal. I have formed a very high opinion of him in every respect and feel the greatest confidence in him.

On 13 August, Rowlands assumed his new command which was to be expanded by the addition of a further battalion of British infantry — Thesiger having ordered the 80th Regiment (2nd Bn South Staffordshire Regiment) to move to Pretoria to release the 1/13th for operations against Sekhukhune.* Captains Clarke (despite his earlier failings) and Carrington were to be given suitable subordinate commands under Rowlands. In a letter to the new Commandant of the Transvaal, Thesiger wrote:

> Should Captain Clarke be able to finish the Sekhukhune affair without any aid from British troops and before the 80th arrive on the scene, it will then be necessary to prepare for the invasion of Zululand.

This comment is important for two reasons. Firstly, it clearly showed Thesiger's intention to invade Zululand several months before events in that region had deteriorated to such an extent as to warrant such action. Secondly, and of more importance in the present context, it indicates the General's lack of understanding of the events and conditions in the Transvaal and in Sekhukhune's country in particular. In Clarke he had an officer who had totally failed to organise any form of effective operation during the preceding months and who had completely lost the support of the local volunteers; he had failed to appreciate the topographical and logistical problems involved in trying to conduct even

---

* *This gave Rowlands a force of some 1,200 infantry and 600 irregular cavalry.*

the simplest of operations in the type of terrain which was to be found in the Lulu mountains. Clarke had, in reality, failed in every aspect of his duties as a field commander.

Rowlands, however, would have to proceed with operations against Sekhukhune whatever the circumstances and did not make the error of underestimating his enemy. He had already toured much of the region in which he would have to operate and believed that success was very unlikely with the forces at his disposal. As August approached its end, he felt that he was as ready to move out of Pretoria as he was ever likely to be. Before leaving, he sent a final note to the Colonial Secretary to the Transvaal government in which he expressed his fears:

> My present strength of mounted volunteers is inadequate for effecting decisive results and a large proportion of these have already tendered their resignation.

The volunteers, by the very nature of their terms of service, were not obliged to take part in the expedition and many felt that in this instance, discretion was by far the better part of valour. One of them, W. H. Tomasson wrote: 'The force at his [ROWLANDS] disposal was quite inadequate to approach Secocoeni's [*sic*] Town'. The luxury of withdrawal from the expedition was not, however, available to Rowlands or the British troops under his command and every opportunity was taken to gain from the expertise of the local population in order to try and eliminate as many of the unknown risks as possible. One such man that Rowlands consulted was a well known and respected Transvaaler named Struben:

> On request I showed Colonel Rowlands and Captain Harvey the map of Sekhukhune's Country, explained the features as to water, roads, the best approaches to the strongholds etc., and specially warned them against taking the advice of Captain Clarke who was then at Fort Burghers, as he had been unfortunate with Sekhukhune and would lead them into difficulties. I knew the country well but was too busy to go myself … I went with the force as far as the lower Elands river, to help them get en route and then returned to Pretoria.

On 28 August, Rowlands led his column out of the Transvaal capital and, following Struben's instructions, travelled up the Elands river to its junction with the Oliphant river where, on 6 September, they met up with Captain Clarke who had ridden out from Fort Weeber to discuss the

The road to Sekhukhune's country. This and the photographs on pages 110 & 111 clearly show the barren nature of the landscape during a summer drought. [H. W. Kinsey]

situation. Struben had advised Rowlands to follow the Oliphant river to its junction with the Steelpoort, north-east of Sekhukhune's territory from where the column was to ascend the valley of the Steelpoort in a SSW direction until it reached Fort Burghers which, at the time, was unoccupied, but could be used as a base for operations against Sekhukhune. The reasoning behind this plan of advance was twofold. Firstly, the entire route followed the course of rivers and it was hoped that, despite the advent of drought in the region, there would be no major shortage of water. Secondly, the route circumnavigated Sekhukhune's Country and therefore did not directly provoke an attack by the Pedi. If, however, such an attack were made, it would have to be launched across a river and would hopefully lack the element of surprise.

On reaching the Oliphant, Rowlands decided to disregard Struben's warning about the consequences of consulting with Clarke and the route of the march was changed. He opted to establish defensive positions on the western side of the Lulu mountains which would pose a threat to the

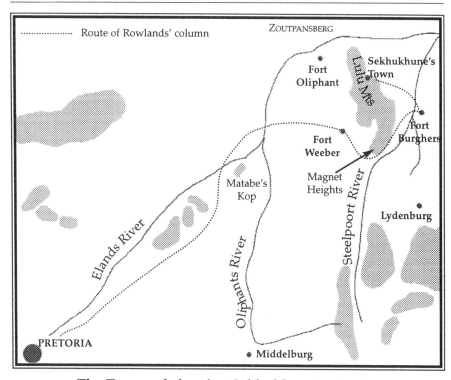

The Transvaal showing Sekhukhune's Country

enemy while the main column would march directly to Fort Burghers, by way of Fort Weeber. This meant that, instead of avoiding Sekhukhune's territory, the column would march straight across it. Rowlands believed that the disadvantages which this imposed were outweighed by the potential advantage of a major saving of time which meant that the column would, hopefully, be less affected by the drought and there would be fewer opportunities for the Pedi to attack before they reached Fort Burghers. Upon reaching their destination, it was planned that Rowlands would lead an attack on the eastern side of the Lulu range and, if possible, advance and destroy Sekhukhune's Town.

The static positions to the west were placed under the overall command of Major England, who had recently arrived in the area from Lydenburg. At the Oliphant river, Rowlands left Captain Waddy with 100 men of the 1/13th Regiment and 40 mounted volunteers, whilst garrisons were also despatched to Fort Mamelube (Captain Thurlow with 50 men of the 1/13th, 40 mounted volunteers and one 4-lb Krupp gun) and Fort Faugh-a-Ballagh (Lieutenant Pollock with 50 men of the 1/13th, 20 mounted volunteers, 100 natives and one 4-lb Krupp gun). The column which Rowlands was left with was a very mixed affair and comprised Captain Riedel's Volunteer Artillery (three Krupp guns and one 6-lb Whitworth gun), Captain Eckersley's Swazis (approximately 200 in number), Van Deventer's Mounted Volunteers, Captain Carrington's Transvaal Mounted Volunteers, a Royal Engineer detachment under the command of Lieutenant MacDowel and several companies of the 1/13th Regiment under the command of Lieutenant Colonel Gilbert.

On 8 September, the column crossed the Oliphants river and proceeded towards Fort Weeber. The drought conditions in the region immediately began to affect the horses but it would appear that the men's spirits were high.

> As sure as eggs are eggs the 13th L .I. will clear his [SEKHUKHUNE'S] stronghold before they return, under two such officers as accompany us, Colonels Rowlands and Gilbert.

On the 10 September, they reached Fort Weeber where they rested for three days before continuing the advance. The nearer they approached Sekhukhune's territory, the more dismal became the terrain and the road became steeper and more rugged as it began to climb towards the Magnet Heights overlooking the valley of the Steelpoort.

> Roads are wretched for travelling, dust over shoetops, and what with the excessive dryness of the weather, many are suffering from tender feet but still march on.

As they neared the Steelpoort river, some of Van Deventer's men spotted large numbers of Pedi warriors (whose fires had been observed during the previous night) ahead of them on a ridge. As soon as the column began to move on the morning of the 14th, the enemy opened a very heavy musket fire on it, but to little effect. Eventually, however, the nuisance effect of the firing increased to such an extent that Rowlands decided to take some action to stop it and a company of the 1/13th,

Facing: Plan of Fort Burghers, 1876. [via H. W. Kinsey]

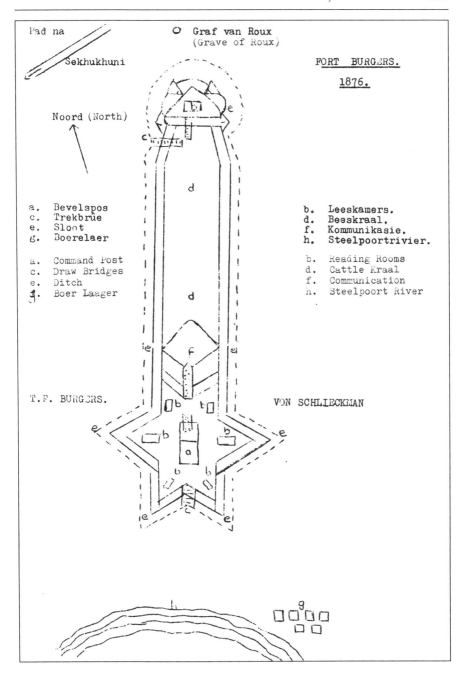

Pad na Sekhukhuni

O Graf van Roux
(Grave of Roux)

FORT BURGERS.

1876.

Noord (North)

a. Bevelspos
c. Trekbrûe
e. Sloot
g. Boerelaer

a. Command Post
c. Draw Bridges
e. Ditch
g. Boer Laager

b. Leeskamers.
d. Beeskraal.
f. Kommunikasie.
h. Steelpoortrivier.

b. Reading Rooms
d. Cattle Kraal
f. Communication
h. Steelpoort River

T.F. BURGERS.

VON SCHLIECKMAN

Above: The site of Fort Weeber. Slight indentations in the ground are all that remain of the fort. [H. W. Kinsey]

Below: Site of Sekhukhune's Town in the foreground. [H. W. Kinsey]

Above and below: The landscape around Sekhukhune's Town. [H. W. Kinsey]

under Captain W. Cox, (later Brevet Major), was present at Kambula where he was severely wounded. the mounted forces and the Swazis were sent to clear the ridge. The infantry advanced in skirmishing order whilst the mounted troops made a flanking move around one of the rock outcrops. As the infantry opened fire the Swazis advanced through the tall grass and rushed the Pedi position, forcing them to retreat. At this point the mounted troops appeared in order to cut off the enemy's withdrawal, but the ruggedness of the terrain made pursuit difficult and the Pedi, unencumbered by heavy equipment, were able to make good their escape.

This brief action had the desired effect of dissuading the Pedi from harassing the column and for the next three days the march passed without further incident as the column stayed as close as possible to the Steelpoort. On the 17 September, as they approached Tolyana Stadt, they again came under inaccurate fire from the heights above them but suffered no casualties. The enemy were so well concealed and so high up that it was decided that any attempt to storm their position would not be worth the effort involved and Van Deventer's men were left behind, in a concealed position, as the remainder of the column continued on its way. No sooner had the main force vacated the camp site than a group of Pedi moved down from the mountain. They were allowed to reach the camp site before the order was given for the hidden troops to open fire. Several Pedi were seen to be hit but the actual losses were not recorded. At Johannes Kop, Captain Carrington and his men were detached from the column and ordered to clear the kraals in the area, which they did without loss.

On leaving the Steelpoort valley, the column met up with Commandant Raaf's Transvaal Rangers and Captain Persse's company of the 1/13th Regiment who were waiting in Waterfall valley. That night, the combined force encamped in the Speckboom valley where they remained for a week in order to allow the commissariat time to catch them up with much needed supplies. On the morning of 24 September, Rowlands, leading part of the column, set out on the last stage of the journey reaching Fort Burghers, some fourteen miles distant, later the same day. The remainder of the column followed three days later, having been reinforced by two detachments of artillery (a mule battery of two 7-lb guns commanded by Lieutenant Frederick Nicolson and two 6-lb guns under the command of Lt. F. G. Slade) and the Frontier Light Horse (consisting of 190 men) under the command of Major Redvers Buller. This brought the total strength of the force at Rowlands' disposal to about 1,300 men.

Fort Burghers had been constructed in 1876 during the abortive assault on Sekhukhune's stronghold by the Transvaal Boers and was situated at the confluence of the Steelpoort and Speckboom rivers. Despite its well-watered position, the fort was an unhealthy outpost and subject to the deadly horse sickness. Nor was the site a good one from a defensive view-point as the fort was hemmed in on one side by the Lulu mountains and on the

Commandant Pieter Raaf.

other by Mount Morone, making it vulnerable to surprise attack. The fort itself was an earthwork construction in the shape of a six-pointed star with an oblong cattle kraal on its north-east side, the far end of which was protected by a smaller defensive work. The whole was surrounded by a ditch which was crossed by means of two drawbridges. It was far from being the ideal situation for Rowlands' column but the plan was that it would only be used as a base from which attacks could be launched into Sekhukhune's territory and that these forays would concentrate all the attention of the Pedi and thereby deter them from making any assault of their own against the fort. With all his force assembled at Fort Burghers, Rowlands gave Lieutenant MacDowel, RE, the task of organising repairs to the defences which, during the previous two years, had suffered damage caused by both the Pedi and the ravages of the elements. Two gun-batteries were sited at the western and eastern sides of the fort respectively and, having secured his base to the best of his ability using the available resources, Rowlands turned his attention to operations against Sekhukhune.

On 26 September, Major Buller and the Frontier Light Horse were sent out on an aggressive reconnaissance into Sekhukhune's territory and returned before nightfall having captured 147 head of cattle for the loss of one man wounded and one horse killed. If the Pedi had been in any doubt as to the intentions of the column, those doubts had now been dispelled.

On 3 October, Rowlands personally led a force of 130 men of the 1/13th, the Frontier Light Horse, a small number of mounted infantry and two 7-lb Krupp guns, out of the fort with the intention of establishing an advanced camp at Marulas Kraal, some fifteen miles to the north-west, from where he could organise raids to weaken and dishearten the enemy.

From the start, however, the plan began to go astray as, before they had covered four miles, they came under fire from Pedi warriors concealed in the rocks above their route of march. Water was in short supply and evidence of horse sickness began to appear almost immediately so that by the end of the first day's march, the force had only covered eight miles and a halt was made at a watercourse which contained a few small pools of water. The following day, in an attempt to cover as much distance as possible before the heat became too great, they resumed their march at 5*a.m.* and managed to advance a further seven miles through some very rough country before setting up their second camp at 3.30*p.m.* near a dry water course. Holes were dug and sufficient water was found for the men, but the animals fared badly as not only did they get little or no water, but the countryside around was denuded of pasture. At 8.00*p.m.*, the Pedi launched an attack against three sides of the camp but the troops, who were well prepared, opened fire and within half an hour the attackers had been driven back. The noise of the fighting, however, caused the animals to stampede and, although search parties managed to locate all the horses, a number of oxen that had been brought along for food were not recovered. The only casualty was one of the volunteer officers, a man named Schulte, who was wounded.

Early the next morning, the column resumed its march and the Pedi again commenced their harassing fire but with little effect. It was believed that there was a supply of water ahead but, on approaching the area, a large number of the enemy were seen to be in positions on the surrounding hills which controlled the pools. Rowlands ordered Raaf's and Van Deventer's men, supported by a company of infantry, to storm one of the hills whilst the Frontier Light Horse, supported by the Swazis, attacked a second and some mounted infantry attempted to clear a third. Supporting fire was to be provided, where necessary, by the mule battery. Before any real contact could be made however, the Pedi fled and the column was ordered to rest and water the animals but, unfortunately, it was discovered that the supplies were limited and the oxen were once again deprived of water. This desperate shortage resulted in Buller and some men of the Frontier Light Horse being sent off to search for alternative supplies and they later returned with the news that there was water some three miles away, situated in a spot which would be suitable for an overnight halt. Rowlands ordered the column forward but, on arriving at the proposed site, discovered that Buller had grossly miscalculated and that what little water there had been had already been consumed by his party. Once again holes were dug but precious little water was found and only one third of the horses received anything at all.

> The sufferings of the 13th Light Infantry on their march was painful to witness and Colonel Rowlands might well say that the game was not worth the candle. Hostilities consisted of marching under a broiling hot sun at the foot of steep mountains whence Basutos fired with such weapons and skill as they possessed.
>
> Fortunately the dangers were small. Why President Burgers got into conflict about such a hopeless country is more than we can discover.

During his reconnaissance, Buller had reached as far as Marulas Kraal and his men had actually opened fire upon the inhabitants before withdrawing. At 4 o'clock the following morning, the whole column headed for the kraal which, as they approached, appeared to be deserted. This was not the case, however, and, once again, the Pedi opened fire on them from the relative safety of the rocks. This fire was returned by all the units in the column. By this time, Rowlands had realised that the column, even if it took the kraal without any losses, could not advance any further as the water shortage was having a serious effect upon the livestock. Indeed, he had made his decision the previous night:

> At sundown I requested the attendance of Captain Clarke, R.A., and assembled the Commanding Officers of Corps. I was comforted to find that

one and all [author's italics] endorsed the opinion that I had already formed, viz that it was impossible for me to effect my object and, that under existing circumstances my only course was to fall back on Fort Burgers.

Although at least one officer later seemed to disagree with this decision, it is of interest to note that at the time Rowlands was clearly under the impression that *all* the senior officers in his command agreed with him. Why, having made such a decision, he still advanced to Marulas Kraal the following morning is something of a mystery. It may have been that it was one last attempt to locate an adequate supply of water which would have enabled the column to continue and, if the kraal had been deserted, they might have been able to remain there long enough to recover their strength. Or, it may have been that Rowlands hoped to demonstrate to the Pedi the strength of his force. Whatever the reason, the decision to advance before finally ordering the withdrawal, is a clear indication that Rowlands was very much against admitting defeat and that if it had been at all possible for him to have continued then he would have done so.

At *6a.m.*, Rowlands ordered the column halt, turn around and head back the way it had come. When they reached the pools where they had halted the previous night, they found them already occupied by a large enemy force. Balancing the desperate need for water against the condition of his men, Rowlands decided that discretion was the better part of valour and by-passed the position and the water. At *4.30p.m.*, after ten hours in the blazing sun, with temperatures reaching 110 degrees Farenheit in the shade, the column reached the water-holes where they had camped on the night of 3 September. Both men and animals were exhausted and a halt was called for the night.

Early the following morning the withdrawal was resumed. The Pedi, anticipating that the soldiers would return by the same route as they had come, gathered to await them, but Rowlands decided to change the route in the hope that they might come across some water and, in doing so, avoided a confrontation. The mounted units were no longer in a condition to be able to ride out far ahead of the infantry as both horses and men were too exhausted. The cattle were almost finished and, indeed, some had already died. One of the volunteers wrote:

... hence our reason for not at once marching to Secocoeni [sic] Town, as we had no reserves to leave in charge of our dying cattle and the wagons and supplies. The position obtained would have been held, despite the overpowering numbers of the enemy, but what would be the use of sacrificing our trek oxen, horses and mules; and mayhap our men would likely succumb for want of water; as it was our cattle were without food for 48 hours. So our Commandant thought, and thought wisely, it was no use attempting to set up camp in this hostile locale until the rainy season sets in.

The previous day, another detachment from Fort Burgers had crossed the Steelpoort river and had established a defensive camp on the western bank. At 7*p.m.* on the evening of 7 October, Rowlands and his men arrived at this new camp where he immediately strengthened the outposts in the hope that Sekhukhune's warriors would follow and attempt to overrun the camp, but they did not appear.

The expedition had been a costly failure; one man wounded, fifteen horses killed or dead from horse sickness, four horses and one mule wounded, as well as the cattle losses which have already been mentioned. The worst casualty however, was the morale of the men which had undergone a severe shaking. Despite the obvious perils of campaigning further south, against the Zulus, one soldier was to write a few weeks later:

> I am glad to have done with Secocoenie [sic] and his rocky mountains and be on the road to Zululand.

As many were to discover during the next few months, campaigning against the Basuto tribes of southern Africa was not going to prove to be the walkover that they had anticipated.

Chapter 10
Tolyana Stadt

The abortive assault on Sekhukhune's mountain stronghold was to have dire consequences for Hugh Rowlands' immediate career and his own personal disappointment at the apparent failure of his first independent active command was to weigh heavily on his mind. In a letter to Sir Theophilus Shepstone he wrote:

> I feel so disappointed that I feel greatly inclined to send in my resignation, although I cannot blame myself for what has occurred. I am only thankful that it did not result in actual disaster.

The British Administrator saw no reason for Rowlands to reproach himself and his reply to the letter did much to raise the latter's spirits so that in his next letter he was in a much more cheerful frame of mind:

> Your kind letter reached me on Monday evening and I thank you very much for it. It acted upon me as oil upon troubled waters and has been the means of alleviating the feelings with which I was harassed, not because I attributed the failure to myself, but to the great disappointment which General Thesiger, yourself and the country at large must experience.

By the end of October, the sense of failure appears to have disappeared almost completely:

> I would be obliged by Your Excellency conveying to Lady Shepstone, with my best respects, my thanks for her kind sympathy. I was very much cut off for some days but the sympathy of others has gone far to remove my affliction.

At this time, Rowlands appears to be the only person suggesting that he might be responsible for the failure of the expedition. That it had an adverse effect upon his abilities as a commander would appear to be in no doubt but, from what documentation that has survived, taken from the writings of the men under his command, there appears to be little evidence that they had lost confidence in him.

We felt much sympathy with Colonel Rowlands who saw himself beaten out of this country by causes utterly beyond his control.

Nor was he criticised by the authorities as witness the comments of Sir Bartle Frere, Governor of Cape Colony:

Colonel Rowlands exercised sound discretion in discontinuing active operations.

General Thesiger was also of the same opinion:

I have every reason to believe that this officer had no option but to retire without attempting an assault on Sekukuni's [sic] Town and I concur with his view of the immediate necessity of withdrawing the mounted portions of his force now horse sickness has broken out.

Perhaps the most informative comment on the abortive assault comes from the regimental history of the 13th Light Infantry in South Africa:

We were all of the opinion in setting out on this expedition against Secocoeni [sic], that it would be an easy matter to put him down; we had, it must be considered, only 600 Imperial forces scattered 40 miles apart, with about 400 Colonial Volunteers and 300 Native Levies. The rebel, it has since been discovered, had more than that number of thousands. It is only necessary to look at the strength of the Imperial forces, which it was found necessary to put him down, close upon 9,000 men on the last expedition.* I have often thought since, I was in luck's way to escape, or so many of us as did.

Within a few days of returning to Fort Burgers, Rowlands had ordered a gradual withdrawal of his force as horse sickness began to sweep through the horses and the cattle; within one week, 115 horses and 50 head of cattle were dead. In stages, the garrison moved up the Spekboom valley and joined up with those units which had been left at the satellite forts some weeks earlier. The men at Fort Faugh-a-Ballagh had been attacked by the Pedi and all travel by day had proved to be too dangerous. On 7 October, the commanding officer, Lieutenant Pollock, had sent a wagon by night under a small escort to Fort Weeber but they had not travelled far before being attacked. In the ensuing fight, Corporal C. Mineary (296), who was in command, was hit by a musket ball which broke his arm and Private J. Doherty (487) was wounded by an assagai. Despite his wound, Doherty managed to defend not only

---

* *Under the command of Sir Garnet Wolseley in 1879.*

himself but also his wounded NCO. Mineary later recovered sufficiently to be able to escape in the darkness and successfully reach Fort Weeber from where relief was sent and the wagon and the remaining men were rescued without further incident.

En route to Fort Faugh-a-Ballagh, Rowlands left a small detachment of the 1/13th at the junction of the Waterfall and Speckboom rivers, with orders to construct a new fort which, due to its close proximity to water, would hopefully be far healthier than Fort Burgers. Officially named Fort Jellalabad (but often referred to as Fort Rowlands) it controlled the road from the Magnet Heights to the Speckboom valley and south to Lydenburg. He hoped that this would be the centre for his second attempt at assaulting Sekhukhune's territory.

Rowlands' plan was to attack the area controlled by the chief Umsoeti at Tolyana Stadt and the forces at his disposal were prepared accordingly. The Frontier Light Horse, which had been sent south from Fort Burgers towards Lydenburg in order to escape the further ravages of horse sickness, was recalled. Four companies of the 80th Regiment were drafted in as reinforcements, three of which were sent to Middleburg, Fort Weeber and Fort Oliphant* thus enabling Captain Waddy's company of the 1/13th to leave the area of the Oliphant river and rejoin the main column. The remaining company of the 80th was posted to Lydenburg with orders to provide supplies for Fort Jellalabad (a detachment of this company was later moved north and stationed at Labuschaignes Farm). Three hundred additional *volunteers* were sent from the Rustenburg District (an action which clearly indicated that Rowlands had not entirely lost the support of the Transvaal population) under the command of Commandant Nel and attached to the main column.

By 2 October, Rowlands was ready to move his re-grouped forces which consisted of six artillery pieces (manned by 48 artillerymen), 1/13th Regiment, 70 mounted infantry, 100 men of the Frontier Light Horse (again commanded by Major Redvers Buller), Raaf's Corps, the Rustenburg Volunteers, 500 natives and 270 horses.

The first day of the march passed without incident but, on 25 October, the enemy showed themselves and in what had now come to be regarded as normal practice, began to fire down from the heights above the column. Captain Otway and half of his company of the 1/13th were ordered to clear them off the hills which they did without loss to themselves and, by the end of the day, the column had reached the Umsoet valley where a camp was established. Captain Carrington, leading some of the volunteers, was ordered out on a reconnaissance and did not return until later in the evening when he had little to report. As the camp settled down, in the last of the daylight, the enemy again showed themselves and began firing and Rowlands ordered Lieutenant Slade, RA, and his two 6-lb Armstrong guns to take up a position on the camp side of the river. All the mounted troops and volunteers and three companies of the 1/13th (under the command of Captains Cox, Waddy and Otway) forded the river under the command of Lieutenant Colonel Gilbert and, on reaching the far side, they moved rapidly up the kop towards the firing. The mounted troops, however, found the slope too steep and were forced to retire to await further orders whilst the infantry continued their climb. Before they could come into contact with the enemy, however, the latter had disappeared into the mountains. Rowlands then withdrew all the troops resolving to continue the pursuit in the morning.

At 4.30*a.m.*, Rowlands personally led the force back across the river and sent the mounted units on ahead to clear the low-lying area and to serve as a shield for the infantry. The previous night, some of the men who had reached the top of kop in pursuit of the enemy had noticed Tolyana's Stadt and it was in that direction that Rowlands now led his column. The artillery were pushed on ahead and took up a position about a mile from the settlement and opened fire with common, double and shrapnel shells, which were effective in clearing all the visible enemy from the encampment and sending them running up the kop in search of cover. Somewhat surprisingly, the attack had caught the Pedi by surprise and Rowlands quickly deployed his men for action. The Swazis, divided into two groups and supported by Captain Otway's company and Raaf's Corps, quickly moved up the northern slopes while three companies of the 1/13th advanced on the settlement itself and came under a very heavy fire from the surrounding heights. The Rustenburg Contingent were sent in support of the Swazis who soon came to grips with the enemy. Intense firing continued for an hour and a half during which time the situation was never very clear but, with the occasional support of the artillery, they were able to drive the Pedi further up the slopes until the latter, seeing themselves in danger of being totally overrun, fled from view.

Rowlands then ordered the destruction of the stadt and the withdrawal of the wounded to the ambulances which were in the rear. No sooner had the troops commenced upon these duties than heavy firing recommenced from an adjacent hill and three companies of the 1/13th were despatched to clear the position. A short time later, Captains Persse and Waddy were able to report that they had taken the position and the artillery was brought to bear on a group of the enemy who were seen to be retreating (estimates were that this group alone numbered some 600 men). Troops were then sent on a 'mopping-up' operation in the surrounding hills and, at 10*a.m.*, Rowlands gave the order to cease firing and recalled all units. As the column commenced to withdraw a few of the enemy reappeared, having no doubt concealed themselves in the caves in the surrounding hills, and once again opened fire, but to no effect.

To have followed up this successful attack with a full-scale pursuit of the retreating native forces would have been a futile and possibly highly dangerous exercise as one of the infantrymen later recorded:

> One thing the attack taught us — the uselessness of pouring lead into these strongholds of natural formation. Fortresses in themselves, from 3 to 500 feet high, formed in places where boulder towers on top of boulder, with massive rocks 40 feet high, affording sufficient cover for hundreds of men. The killed and wounded of the enemy were estimated at 600.

There can be little doubt that this operation was a great morale booster for both Rowlands and the men under his command. His losses had been low, eight British soldiers wounded* (one of whom, Colour Sergeant John Pegg , 1/13th, died on 28 October and became the first British soldier to be killed on active service in the Transvaal), and four natives wounded. The column also captured 38 head of cattle and 30 goats. Rowlands was obviously delighted when he published his orders on 28 October:

Of these only Colour Sergeant Pegg, Bugler G. Burge (100) — slightly wounded in the thigh — and Privates T. Emery (1637) slightly wounded, J. Merryweather (1956) dangerously wounded and F. Smith (1919) slightly wounded, all of the 1/13th Regiment, can be identified.

The Commandant desires to express his satisfaction at the conduct of all who took part in the attack on Tolyana Stadt yesterday ... [he] congratulates the forces engaged upon the small number of casualties which took place, considering the great natural strength and intricate nature of the enemy's position but regrets the death of Colour-Sergeant Pegg.

Rowlands had intended '... to show Sekhukhune that their strong places were accessible to us, did we chose to attack them, and [he] put the red coats in the van that they should not say it was done by natives'. In this object he was successful and, having regrouped his forces, he ordered their return to Fort Burgers where a detachment under the command of Captain W. H. Evans and Lieutenant R. Levinge was serving as a garrison. The Frontier Light Horse made its way to Lydenburg with orders to proceed from there to Utrecht.

By this time, war with the Zulus seemed inevitable and Rowlands received a letter from Thesiger recommending that he withdrew all his forces from Sekhukhune's country and concentrate them on the two roads leading to Middleburg and Pretoria. All the surviving evidence would indicate that this instruction was given, not as a direct order, but more as a suggestion. Even had it been an order, it was somewhat vague in that it only gave the withdrawal point as the general position of the two roads. This presented Rowlands with a problem as, during the time he had been at Fort Burgers, several of the local tribes had given him their active assistance which meant that, if he now withdrew, Sekhukhune would almost certainly seek his revenge. Not only would this be gross betrayal by an ally but, would also create problems for any future force entering the area hoping for the co-operation of the local population against Sekhukhune; British power in Pretoria, or even at Fort Weeber, was very distant and theoretical, whereas Sekhukhune's was very near and very real. Another consideration was the view held by the British Commissioner for Zoutpansberg, Sir Morrison Barlow, that any drastic withdrawal of British troops would seriously jeopardise the security of the district, so much so that it might become necessary to evacuate the town of Esteling which action would do serious damage to future British credibility. Finally, Rowlands had to consider the volunteer troops under his command. The General had suggested that, after the withdrawal of the British troops, the security of the area could be placed in the hands of the volunteers and native levies. Rowlands, as the man on the spot, considered this to be a grave miscalculation as the volunteers had suffered a severe blow to their morale during the course of the year and the general consensus was '... that volunteers will not serve here'. As far as the native levies were concerned, it was felt that they could not reasonably be expected to serve without the direct support of British troops.

Thesiger saw the role of the Imperial troops in the area, after this withdrawal, to be that of containing Sekhukhune and his warriors inside his territory. If this could be successfully carried out then the Pedi would be unable to leave the mountains to plant their crops for the following season and it was anticipated that this would cause their chief such problems that many of his people would desert him with the result that another campaign might prove unnecessary. Such a view can, at best, be seen as naïve and, at worst, downright foolish, as there was little evidence to suggest that such an action would do anything other than provoke the Pedi to take action. Thesiger's education in the ways of the native tribes of southern Africa was lacking in many areas but he was to learn the error of his views in the very near future at an enormous cost in lives to both Imperial and volunteer troops.

When Rowlands had weighed up all the factors, he decided to withdraw his forces to six stations, each of which was to be garrisoned by one company of the 80th Regiment, a plan which was supported by others present in the Transvaal, notably Shepstone, Barlow and Clarke. When news of these dispositions reached Thesiger in Pietermaritzburg, the reaction was quite different. The General was furious and communicated his views to both Rowlands and Shepstone:

1. I have written to Sir Theophilus Shepstone to say I am not at all satisfied with your proposed distribution of the 80th Regiment.

2. I object most emphatically to their being left in small detachments to occupy positions where they cannot act offensively and where they are liable to insult — I trust the Administrator will agree with me and that you will receive my letter to him endorsed with his approval.

3. On receipt of it kindly carry out at once the concentration of the companies of the 80th on the two roads.

4. The security of the inhabitants must be given to the volunteers and native levies.

5. You had better place Captain Clarke in command of all the volunteer and native levies and come back yourself to Middelburg where you will be nearer this place. Abandon all idea of any further movements against Sekhukhune and his supporters and consider yourself at my disposal for work on the Zulu border.

In a second letter, dated the same day, Thesiger wrote 'The distribution you sent me for approval is drastically opposed to the one I sent you for your guidance.' The word 'guidance' in this sentence seems to be all important, for he is reinforcing the assumption that his earlier communication had not been an order and yet he was now castigating Rowlands for not carrying out his instructions. As it transpired, Shepstone did not agree with the General but failed to do anything to substantially support Rowlands' position. It was obvious that Thesiger saw the activities in the northern Transvaal as unnecessary distractions to the main event which was about to take place further south in Zululand and any deviation from his plans would only serve to direct much needed resources elsewhere.

This reaction from Thesiger brought with it the return of Rowlands' depression. He was meant to be operating as an independent field commander and yet he was being controlled by a senior officer who was not only remote from the scene of activity, but who appeared to have no appreciation of either the situation or the conditions in the Transvaal. Since Rowlands had abandoned the assault on Sekhukhune's Town (which the General had publicly declared was the result of problems over which any local commander had no control) he felt that he had conducted operations in a competent and professional manner and, as a result, had achieved a small measure of success against the enemy. The appointment of Captain Clarke of all people to command the volunteers and natives, and his own withdrawal from the north-eastern Transvaal, could only be viewed as a criticism of his handling of the situation. On 2 December, he wrote to Shepstone:

I am naturally very grieved at what has occurred but I don't see that I could possibly have acted otherwise. Had I been told that it was necessary for the service that I should remain in command of the N.E. frontier because the exigencies of the service required it, I could not have objected, and would, as always have obeyed orders, however distasteful it would have been to have been debarred from taking part in the Zulu War. But to be deprived of the command of a Field Column and substituted by a junior in rank for no

Major Redvers Buller.

apparent reason than a misinterpretation of orders, indicates that it is time to withdraw from the position in which I am placed. It is just possible that the General may reconsider his determination when he hears that his orders have been fully carried out, but I do not think its likely. Neither do I think that he will sanction my application, until such times as he may be able to replace me.

However, I have known General Thesiger for a long time, and I feel sure he has acted with conscientious motives in this matter, from which the veil of mystery may in time be removed.

It is a sad blow but I cannot condemn myself for acting in any way otherwise that what I consider to be for the best and I doubt not that the gradual withdrawal consequent upon a misinterpretation of orders has been really more productive of good, than a hasty and precipitated evacuation of the enemy's territory might have been.

These were clearly the words of a very disillusioned man. Rowlands evidently felt the situation in which he found himself to be intolerable and had offered Thesiger his resignation. The General declined to accept it and asked him to reconsider:

> I have written to Colonel Rowlands telling him he must not resign. It would be ruination to him from a professional point of view.

Once again, the ambiguity of the General's style of command becomes clear in a letter which he wrote, on the same day, to Shepstone:

> As an independent Field Commander he [Rowlands] is a failure, but I will not put him in such a position again. I hear that he sits in his tent and writes all day. This will not do in South African warfare — a commander must ride about and see the country himself or he will never be able to handle his troops properly.

If Thesiger felt this way then he should have accepted Rowlands' resignation irrespective of the consequences; to do otherwise would be to court disaster should troops be sent into action under his command. The General believed that Rowlands had lost the confidence of the men under his command but what little evidence that has survived does not appear to bear this out. So where did Thesiger get the information which led him to this conclusion? Evidence would suggest that it came from one of two individuals, namely Major Redvers Buller or Captain Clarke. The latter's relative isolation in the Transvaal would appear to rule him out, although Rowlands was certainly concerned that his actions had done little to improve the situation. Buller, however, was in a different situation for, after the action at Tolyana's Stadt, the Frontier Light Horse had left the area and moved to Utrecht from where its commander had written to his close friend Colonel Evelyn Wood, VC:

> Oh! for an hour of [—]
> or well brained word to lead the fight
> and quit us of this Rowlands wight [sic]
> who does not understand its quits
> To smash this Sekukuni [sic].

You must allow me just once to say — Damn that Rowlands — There, I am better now, a little better, fancy. Here I have been for a month, what have I done 'nothing'. What had anybody done, nothing. Yes we have though we have let the Kaffirs get cheeky, and now we are bolting — Between you and me my dear and please, keep it dark, Rowlands is quite useless. He cannot make up his mind to anything, sitting on his behind in this position and Harvey, unfortunately is worse, much more than useless for he possesses the same faults as Rowlands and to an aggravated degree … I even wished you had been here — Joking apart, I do wish you had, I feel sure we should have tried something and usually to try means to do, but this idiot didn't try — just sits on his behind, that's his form, a charming man he is too, so nice, but I would rather be cursed by someone who would do something.

We have nearly 500 horsemen at Fort Burgers for a month, what have we done —I have done two patrols and both these I had to … ask leave to go on — Now, just as he has made up his mind to bolt and give up, he has been persuaded to do what I suggested three weeks ago, and the cause of this letter is that I am out of it. Hard case. B bullies R for 3 weeks to attack Umsoeti's Kraal. R cannot make up his mind — R sends B away because his horses are dying and then makes up his mind to attack — B is consequently out of the fight.

What should B do —
Answer adjudged correct — Curse R! And I have done it my dear E. I can tell you. I have written him such a letter, that I fully expect he will change his mind again and send me an order to rejoin him.[4]

Strong words indeed from a subordinate about his commanding officer and, at face value, they appear to condemn Rowlands as a man who was totally unfit to hold his command and it would appear that Thesiger's opinion was well founded upon fact. It is almost certain that it was Buller's attitude which was the root cause of the General's revised attitude towards Rowlands and one can assume, with a degree of confidence, that either Buller wrote himself to Thesiger or else Evelyn Wood did so upon receipt of the above letter. Later events were to suggest that it was probably the latter who was responsible.

Buller and Wood were amongst the élite of British army officers during the 1870s both having shot to fame under the guidance of Sir Garnet Wolseley, the most influential general in the army, a man with his eyes set upon the highest office, that of Commander-in-Chief. They had come together in Ashanti in 1873–4, where Wolseley had his first independent command and had gathered around him a group of promising young officers who were nicknamed 'The Ring' and who were much resented by those outside of the circle. As Wolseley's star began its ascent, these officers followed and eventually rose to high office themselves. This is not meant to imply that these men were lacking in ability, far from it, and both Buller and Wood had already shown themselves to be outstanding officers en route to the commands which they held in 1878. Wood already held the Victoria Cross and Buller was to receive one the following year.

It is of interest to briefly examine the personality of Redvers Buller who was seen as the wild man of the British Army and then perhaps to view the above letter in that light. The second son of a wealthy Devon squire, Buller had been expelled from Harrow School and completed his education at Eton before being commissioned into the 60th Rifles in 1858. His courage was well known and verged on sheer rashness: 'He may have known the meaning of the word fear, but there was no evidence that he ever let it influence his conduct and he had no tolerance for it in others'. Biographer Julian Symonds described him as 'brave to the point of insanity, not the sort of man to turn back'. He was a superb horseman and his endurance in the saddle enabled him to ride most men into the ground. He was a heavy drinker, foul tempered and prone to the use of violence in order to get his own way. As a junior officer, he made a very unfavourable impression upon those whom he met, 'they found him a country clodhopper, raw and brash, and a clodhopper who did not acknowledge inferiority, but having once got an idea into his bullet head, argued interminably for it, unmoved by the fact that he was contradicting his seniors. His powers of administration and organisation were low, his grasp of strategy even lower. He was vociferous rather than articulate,

Lt. Colonel Evelyn Wood, VC

and his positive manner masked the fact that what he said and wrote was not always what he had in his mind. He was also indecisive.'

In 1879, the Zulu War was to bring Buller's name to the attention of the entire nation and he became known as the 'Bayard of South Africa'. In action he seemed to the Zulus to be some sort of evil spirit '... as he led his men at a swinging canter, his reins in his teeth, a revolver in one hand and a knobkerry in the other, his face streaked with blood.' Command of the Frontier Light Horse suited him perfectly as the men under his command were, on the whole, undisciplined volunteers and his unconventional nature and appearance endeared him to them to such an extent that they would follow him anywhere. He was as different from Rowlands as chalk is from cheese and they might have made a better team twenty-five years earlier when Rowlands was a far younger, more foolhardy, independent spirit who thirsted for action. The intervening years had mellowed Rowlands' attitude towards combat and had also given him considerable experience of command — a factor already recognised by Thesiger. From his earliest days in the army, he had concerned himself with the well-being of those who served under him. Buller however, if his letter to Wood is by any means an accurate reflection of his outlook, appears to have been only worried about himself and the personal glory which he might collect. He seems to have had little grasp of the overall military situation in the Transvaal. At no time does he make any reference to why Rowlands failed to take up his suggestions and he seems to have been totally unaware of the part which Thesiger played in the restriction of Rowlands' actions in the Transvaal. For a man who professed such a knowledge of horses, Buller's attitude towards the outbreak of horse-sickness borders on the insane. Indeed, from the tone of his letter it would appear that his 'suggestions' were very close to insubordination rather than constructive comments. Even the literary style of the letter leads one to question the suitability of the writer to hold a position of authority. Rowlands had ample reason for being wary of Buller's opinion as a major part of the problem which he had faced whilst advancing towards Sekhukhune's Town was the shortage of water caused by the poor reconnaissance work and lack of discipline of the Frontier Light Horse. When the column was forced to return to Fort Burgers, the decision was only made after Rowlands had consulted with all the unit commanders involved and that presumably included Buller. Rowlands recorded that '… one and all endorsed the opinion that I had already formed'. It is on record that the drought of 1878 was without precedent and those in high authority fully accepted Rowlands' decision to abandon the operation and it would appear that Buller's was the only voice which was raised in protest.

Buller's opinion of Captain Harvey was also grossly inaccurate for, after the end of the hostilities in the Transvaal, Harvey was appointed Brigade Major of the 1st Brigade, 1st Division during the second advance into Zululand and was later appointed Deputy Assistant Quartermaster General to the 1st Division. At the end of the Zulu War he was rewarded with a Brevet Majority for his services in southern Africa; hardly the type of career advancement given to a total incompetent!

There can be little doubt, however, that Rowlands' actions may have appeared hesitant and over cautious to a man of Buller's temperament but, as later events were to clearly show, this cannot be seen as a failing when campaigning against native forces in the region. Unfortunately for Rowlands, this was a lesson which many had yet to learn and it was to be his downfall as Thesiger had already made up his mind as to his future:

I feel that I have no right to keep from you [Shepstone] what has been gradually forcing itself upon my mind viz —that Colonel Rowlands does not possess the requisite qualifications of an independent commander of Troops in the Field. Knowing as I did what an excellent commanding officer of a regiment he has shown himself to be and that his wearing the Victoria Cross was a sufficient proof of his physical courage, I assumed, wrongly, I regret to say, that his moral courage would not be wanting, and that therefore all these qualities combined with a pleasant manner and gentlemanlike instincts would make him all that Your Excellency or that I could desire. The one weak link in the chain however, want of moral courage, had destroyed the whole combination and has produced failure where I had every expectation of success. Looking to the lateness of the season when the British troops moved into Sekukuni's country; but what I deplore is that the troops under Colonel Rowlands' command should have lost confidence in their commander. I propose to leave Colonel Rowlands in command, as active operations on any side must now necessarily cease – as so far as the administrative duties are concerned he will do them well enough.

By way of a side note to this affair, one cannot help but wonder what may have passed through Buller's mind twenty-one years later when, as a Lieutenant General, he commanded the British forces against the Boers. At Spion Kop he was accused of hesitation, lack of decisiveness, failure to pursue an advantage and was accused of spending all day in his tent when he should have been out trying to salvage something out of a disaster. As a consequence of his inactivity, several thousand lives were lost before he was relegated to a lesser command and his career effectively came to an end. In 1901, in the backwash of the Boer War he was relieved of his command and retired from active service.

Sir Theophilus Shepstone was, however, not of the same opinion with regard to Rowlands' abilities, but was in no position to intervene with the decisions of Thesiger to whom he wrote on 23 November:

I am heartily sorry, as I am sure you are, that you have been obliged to adopt the conclusion you have; his [Rowlands] difficulties have … been very great; and I should urge these on his behalf if it were not for the fatal fact you mention, and which I was not aware of, that he has lost the confidence of his men.

This letter is highly illuminating as Shepstone resided in Pretoria and had worked directly with Rowlands. All movements of officers and men to and from Rowlands' command was carried out via that place and yet no word appeared to have reached the Administrator that Rowlands had lost the confidence of his men. Surely, if there was anything like a sizeable feeling about Rowlands' abilities as a field commander, Shepstone would have heard of it. He wrote to Rowlands:

> I need not assure you how sorry I am at the relations that seem to have sprung up between the General and you; and at the view you take of them; and I shall be still more sorry if you carry out your threat of resigning. You have had a most difficult task to perform and have had to contend against the elements, which display superhuman odds against merely mortal efforts.

He also wrote to Sir Bartle Frere in Cape Town:

> I am sorry to find that Colonel Rowlands has sent his resignation to the General he will be a loss to the Transvaal just now.

What part had Captain Clarke played in this drama? Certainly, due to Clarke's experience in the area, Rowlands appears to have placed a great deal of reliance upon his opinion. As we have already seen, Struben had warned Rowlands against doing such a thing before the latter had left Pretoria and the pioneer and Rowlands met up again some time later at a ball given by Colonel Brooke. When Struben mentioned that his warning had been ignored by Rowlands, the latter replied, 'Please do not say anything about it, I have paid heavily for it'. No further explanation was given for this statement although an interesting comment on Clarke, and perhaps the whole incident in the Transvaal, was published later that year by Captain Aylmer of the Lydenburg Volunteer Corps:

> Clarke wasted opportunities to crush Sekukuni [sic] ... Her Majesty's troops have now been ordered to the front — now when the sickly season is at hand. If Sekukuni does not give in before mid-summer, many an English mother will have to mourn a son. Why was this not done sooner? The reason is not far to seek. Official jealousies and the desire for self-aggrandisement let the opportunity for real work slip past.

Despite this comment on Clarke, Aylmer makes no such judgement about Rowlands and neither does he suggest that the Colonel had lost the confidence of his command.

Whatever the reason, whether justified or not, at the end of 1878, Hugh Rowlands' career was at its lowest ebb but the events in the Transvaal were about to fade into obscurity as the problems facing the army in Zululand came into focus. This moved the spotlight away from Rowlands and gave him the opportunity to salvage something from what appears to have been a disastrous situation.

Chapter 11
Talako Mountain

Towards the end of 1878, Thesiger (who had become the 2nd Baron Chelmsford on the death of his father) was busy with the preparations for the invasion of Zululand. He divided his forces, which consisted of Imperial, volunteer and native troops, into five columns which he stationed along the Zulu frontier. Despite the General's grave misgivings about his abilities, Hugh Rowlands was placed in command of N° 5 Column and ordered to move his head-quarters to Luneburg, a town north of the Pongolo river, near the junction of the Zulu/Swazi borders. It was proposed that the invasion would take place in January when three columns would cross the border into Zululand whilst N° 2 Column (commanded by Colonel Durnford) and N° 5 Column remained at their bases to prevent any Zulu breakout into British territory and also to prevent any other tribes moving south in support of the Zulu king, Cetshwayo. These duties were, in Rowlands' case, to be carried out with reduced forces as Chelmsford detailed in a letter:

> Thanks for your letter of 25th December, received two days ago. I am glad you were able to send some companies to Derby, it will go a long way towards reassuring the Swazis ... You are quite right in mounting the 18 men at Lydenburg. If a pressure arises you are at liberty to send a company to Fort Weeber but I would rather keep all the companies together if possible, and let the volunteers look after that part. If you send them anywhere I would prefer that you send them to Derby ... If you reinforce Derby, kindly go there yourself for a little.

This letter again illustrates Chelmsford's method of command. Instead of issuing direct orders to his subordinate officers, he makes suggestions which, if not carried out, leave the subordinate officer open to criticism. Interestingly, the General no longer seems opposed to the dispersal of the troops in the Transvaal and his comments appear to vindicate

Rowlands' earlier views regarding the attitude of the native tribes to a total withdrawal of British troops from the region.

On 11 January, operations against the Zulus commenced and the three invading columns crossed the frontier without major incident. All concerned expected the campaign to be of a short duration and decisive. Rowlands, meanwhile, was involved in negotiations with the Swazis with a view to enlisting a native army which could be sent into Zululand in support of the regular forces and was out of touch with the operations further south until, on 26 January, he received a letter from Shepstone:

Lt. General Lord Chelmsford.

The General has met with a very severe reverse. It appears that he marched the main body of his column away from his camp in search of an enemy that was not found but which, in the meantime, attacked his camp, scattered and killed most of the defenders, four companies of Col. Pulleine's Regiment, one of the 24th, and sacked the camp … Col Pulleine and all the officers with those soldiers were killed and it is said that only sixty soldiers escaped and they only to be most likely overtaken at Helpmakaar where it is said the enemy pressed on for.

This was the disastrous battle at Isandlwana and, apart from a few details, Shepstone's information was correct. A large part of N° 3 Column had been wiped out and the whole situation changed for the worse.

Despite this reverse (which all the native tribes would undoubtedly have already heard of), Rowlands succeeded in obtaining the promise of support from the Swazi king and the reassurance that any Swazi warriors that were sent could be used as and where the British saw fit. The disaster at Isandlwana, however, dashed any hopes that Rowlands may have had of marching across the Pongolo river and on into

Zululand and he feared for the repercussions amongst the tribes in the Transvaal, not least among the Pedi.

Chelmsford then gave Evelyn Wood, who was in command of N° 4 Column operating in northern Zululand, new powers and informed him by letter of his new status in relation to Rowlands who, by length of service and time in his present rank, was Wood's superior officer.

> I am writing to him [Rowlands] to say that he must be guided entirely by the information and advice you send him as to his movements. I am quite unable to say what he can do and you are the only person who really understands the situation … Kindly send Rowlands full instructions and remember he is on no account to interfere with your independence, but may act as to assist you in such a way as you may advise him.

Rowlands was now in a dilemma. As Commandant of the Transvaal he was the servant of two masters, Chelmsford and Shepstone, which meant that he had to decide whether the security of the Transvaal was his main concern or whether his primary duty was to support Wood's column which was advancing inside Zululand. The course of events did little to assist him in reaching any form of conclusion as he wrote to Shepstone:

> This sad disaster, so unlooked for, may so change the nature of hostilities on the northern border as to at once require the presence of this force on that side and I am of the opinion that it should be kept intact and not used to reinforce other columns.

As if to add to the problems facing the authorities in the Transvaal, the defeat at Isandlwana stirred the local Boers to unrest and they in their turn seized the opportunity to stir up the native population of the area. Piet Joubert, a prominent Boer leader, said in a speech at the end of January, 'If the Zulus enter Natal and kill every Englishman, woman and child I shall say that the Lord is righteous!' The Boers demanded that the British should leave the Transvaal and it was strongly hinted that their failure to do so could well result in an armed rebellion. Rowlands knew that his command was too weak to be effective in Zululand but felt certain that it could be used to maintain the security of the Transvaal and, in the absence of direct orders from Chelmsford, decided to try and maintain the independence of his command inside the region. His predicament is clearly evident in a letter which he wrote to Shepstone on 12 February:

I really don't know what I am considered to do. I have no information whatever from Headquarters to guide me in any way, no hint even … This may be consequent upon the disaster, so as I have said before, I am quite in the dark and puzzled what to do and I think, taking it all round, am very unfairly treated and I feel it deeply. I have met the General's wishes in every way, even the waving of Seniority and taking orders from a junior [viz Wood].

Shepstone was in full agreement with Rowlands and did his utmost, in his opinion, to support him. Chelmsford and Wood however, held other views. The General regarded Rowlands' decision as yet another example of his failure as an independent commander and the tone of his letters altered dramatically. He wrote to Wood:

> I should feel most uncomfortable if I thought you were in any way hampered by the presence of Col. Rowlands … and I am quite prepared to order him away if you find him a nuisance.

Wood's role in this affair, and the events of the closing weeks of 1878, are of interest and some of his correspondence is most illuminating. In a letter to Chelmsford, he wrote, 'I can't find words to express my opinion of Colonel Rowlands' indecision'. In a letter to Rowlands, however, he adopted a very different attitude:

> Allow me to congratulate you on your success of the 15th inst. as regarding your objection to parting with the Transvaal Rangers and mounted men generally. I should like to explain to you that I have always advocated the merging of these two forces into one — and when the 13th Inf. first came down I wrote to the General pointing out the desirability of our merging and suggesting that you should be sent to take command over me. The General I believe wishes you to be kept available for work in the Transvaal but he never gave me reasons, nor answered my questions.

Wood's chameleon-like qualities appear to have stood him in good stead throughout his career and they certainly reinforce the suggestion that there was a great deal of political manoeuvring taking place amongst the senior officers in the region at this time. The main focus of attention and the arena for political manoeuvring was far away from the Transvaal and Rowlands was unaware of what was going on behind his back and had little time to become involved as events in his area of authority suddenly took on an urgency of their own.

By late January, Wood's N° 4 Column was operating from Kambula some 30 miles east of Utrecht. From there, Buller's Frontier Light Horse carried out a series of raids which rapidly enhanced his reputation as a man of action. One of his officers wrote of him:

He would do some dashing act like burning of the Makulusini military kraal, an exploit hardly heard of at home; with a small force of 120 men the colonel burnt a large kraal in face of an enemy several times as numerous; its opponents were a regular drilled regiment, but he brought off his force without any loss of life. It was a sight to see him standing on some eminence in the hottest fire, calmly looking through his telescope.

On 10 February, Buller raided the Hlobane area, destroying huts and capturing cattle, driving the enemy back into his mountain stronghold. But this was a tactical withdrawal. By day, the enemy lay concealed amid the rocks but by night they ventured down to attack isolated settlements and committed what were described as 'barbarous outrages' against natives who were friendly to the British authorities — as Rowlands had predicted some weeks previously. The hornets' nest which had been stirred up by the numerous military raids was now in danger of becoming a major problem for the British authorities. To add to the difficulties many of the volunteers serving under British command were coming to the end of their agreed period of service. Even Buller was unable to persuade over seventy of his Frontier Light Horsemen to sign on again. Undeterred, he led his much depleted force against Manyanyoba's stronghold where he divided his force into two groups and launched an attack during which five Zulu positions were taken and thirty-four Zulus killed. He then withdrew to Luneburg, taking with him a large number of captured cattle with the intention of returning to Eloya mountain the following day in order to finish the task and totally remove the threat. When he was informed that Rowlands was returning from an action at Tolaka mountain and intended to move against other dissident tribes in the region, Buller decided to abandon his plans. It is evident that assaults by under-strength forces against prepared enemy positions would be futile in this campaign. Far better to wait until the attacking force had sufficient strength to assault, seize and hold a position than to merely annoy the enemy and give him more than just cause to seek revenge.

On 12 February, Jacobus Potgieter had been at his farm some ten miles from Tolaka mountain in the company of five other Boer farmers, at the southernmost tip of the Bougane Range when some of his native servants rushed up to the house to inform him that there were large numbers of Zulus gathered on the mountain. Early the following morning, Potgieter and his friends set out to check this report but, due to the thick mist, they found it impossible to see any distance during the first part of the morning and were obliged to advance 'blind' towards the mountain. Eventually, the mist cleared and the small party found itself surrounded by a sizeable force of Zulus who immediately opened fire. The Boers returned the fire and, although very heavily outnumbered, were, as a result of their superior marksmanship, able to gain the upper hand and the Zulus withdrew further up the mountain leaving behind twenty-three dead. Three of Potgieter's natives were also killed. The party then descended the mountain and made its way to Derby where they reported the incident to Rowlands who immediately called up troops and, the same day, led a column towards Tolaka mountain.

Rowlands' force consisted of Captain Harvey, C. A. Potter (acting as guide and interpreter), Jacobus Potgieter and eight other Boers, Raaf's Horse, 103 Transvaal Rangers, 240 of Fairlie's Kaffirs and 75 members of Voss' Kaffirs. En-route, they had some difficulty with two ambulance wagons which accompanied them and so they did not reach Potgieter's Farm until 3*a.m.* on the morning of the 14 February. Rowlands rested his men at the farm for twenty-four hours and, after being joined by Field Cornet Lasbuschagna's Native Force, began to move towards Tolaka mountain, leaving the ambulances behind. Five hours later, as the column approached the lower slopes, they spotted Zulu scouts above them.

> On reaching which [Tolaka mountain] I found it terminates in a precipitous krantz below, in parts a sort of small terrace, then a precipitous fall to the valley of the Pongolo. Here were two kraals of cattle, almost 500 yards apart, the krantz about midway was intersected by a grassy slope which reached to the lower fall of the valley.

Rowlands decided that Potgieter's and Lasbuschagna's men should attack the left gully while Raaff's Horse moved into the right gully. Potter offered to lead the left attack.

Everything went according to plan. The native troops, contrary to expectation, fought well and Rowlands, Harvey and the Boers were able to remain on the upper slope from where they could observe the action. Potter and some of his natives disappeared from view but, even then, the sound of a fierce struggle could clearly be heard for some minutes before they reappeared near the cattle kraals on the lower terrace. One large Zulu, an Induna named Magalini, who had only arrived from Zululand the previous day, could be seen attacking Potter with an assagai but, before he could close his attack, the scout had fired, hitting him in the head. His death seemed to have an adverse effect upon the other Zulus and Potter leapt onto a rock and signalled to Rowlands to send support. Fairlie's Kaffirs, led by Captain Newman and a lieutenant, were ordered into the fight but, as they rushed down the slope they could see that the battle was already over and, by the time they had reached Potter, his men had captured 200 cattle, 80 goats and 44 sheep from the most northerly of the two kraals. Eight Zulu bodies were found in the open but one of those taken prisoner stated that he had seen ten killed in the cave where he was sheltering. In addition to the prized livestock, Potter's men also captured forty-four women and children. Rowlands' losses had been slight: six men wounded and one horse killed. Potter and his men were now anxious to move on and seize the second kraal but Rowlands decided against it as he explained to Shepstone:

> … as I had no means of carrying my wounded a distance of 20 miles to this camp [Luneberg] I did not attack the 2nd kraal which would have been a more difficult task. Arrived in camp 7.30*p.m.* 17th. I had to call a halt on account of heavy rain on the 15th when I marched about eight miles and encamped a mile this side of Uyers Mission Station. I was all day getting over that small distance owing to the rottenness of the transport gear, bad drivers and the loss of some of the foreloopers, who bolted directly the order for the march was issued. I consider my transport under the new regime as defective.

Before leaving the area, Rowlands ordered the burning of all the Zulu buildings, kraal and stores and, en-route for Luneburg, he destroyed many acres of crops which he thought might prove to be of value to the Zulus. On arriving at Luneburg, the column joined up with the remainder of Rowlands' force, comprising the 80th Regiment (under the command of Major Charles Tucker) which had arrived from Derby. But any plans to use the enhanced force to return to the Tolaka area had already been dashed; on the road from Tolaka to Luneburg Rowlands had received a 'request' from Wood for Raaff's Corps to join N° 4 Column without delay. Furious at this further diminution of his forces Rowlands vented his feelings in a letter to Shepstone:

... so here I am after getting a small column together with much difficulty, obliged to part with my mounted men, without whom I cannot operate efficiently in this country. Of course, I cannot decline to comply with the order but it must be apparent to Your Excellency that their withdrawal to another column takes them out of hand for the meeting of pressure on the northern border should they be required. There is much to be done in the Intombe valley and Bellina Berg right away to the White river in the way of clearing out kaffirs and destroying crops. The action taken by the General in taking away my mounted men frustrates my effecting this clearance, and as I said before renders me altogether inefficient. It is not wise or prudent to move with infantry alone, you are never secure without mounted escorts. For considerable numbers can come over occasionally from the right side of the Pongolo, as was the case when Mr Potgieter came in to report to me. He said, and 5 others corroborated what he stated, that he saw at least 400 together, and who tried to surround them. The prisoner also said that the impi had left the kranz the night before I arrived there.

Soon after this a further message arrived from Wood, ordering Rowlands to send Colonel Weatherley's Corps to join N° 4 Column. The departure of this unit left the Transvaal without any organised mounted troops (the Frontier Light Horse being already under the command of N° 4 Column) which meant that Rowlands was unable to take any offensive action against the Zulus and all plans to return to Tolaka mountain were postponed, much to the disgust of the Boers. In March, an unsigned letter appeared in *The Times of Natal* which, although it did not name the person that the author held responsible for the withdrawal and lack of activity, would appear to be a criticism of Chelmsford and Wood rather than Rowlands who had no say in the matter.

... had the success [of the first assault on Tolaka mountain] been followed up this nest of thieves and murderers would have been cleared out; instead of which the road to Derby from Luneburg has been, and continues to be, impassable without a strong military convoy and on several occasions both convoys and others have been fired upon from the mountains and the Zulus are daily increasing.

Contrary to much that has subsequently been written about these events in early February, Rowlands' decision not to return appears, for once, to have the support of his superior officers and the whole attack and tactics used at Tolaka mountain earned him his only independent Mention in Despatches for this period.

Despite the obvious disadvantages which his column was labouring under after the loss of the mounted forces, Rowlands refused to abandon all his plans to strike at the enemy. On 20 February, he received news that a small force of Zulus had been left in charge of supplies at Makatees Kop, a natural fortress near Eloya mountain which, it was believed, the Zulus intended to use as a depot for future operations. The place was believed to be a difficult one to attack and several officers tried to dissuade Rowlands from ordering an assault. Perhaps driven on by the criticism which he had received, he would not be deterred and immediately sent out a detachment as an advanced guard and reconnaissance party. By first light on 20 February, this small force (led by Captain Harvey) had reached one of the border mission stations which consisted of a laager constructed of stones on the bank of a river. Harvey encamped there and later that day was joined by another column led by Rowlands.

During the night, the sentries roused the camp having heard noises from beyond the perimeter but it was a false alarm and they discovered that the sounds had come from a group of Boers returning from Luneburg. These travellers informed Rowlands that the kraal he was looking for was some twenty miles away and was guarded by some fifty Zulus of Nkobamakosi's regiment which was part of the Royal Corps. The number of cattle in the kraal was small but reports said that they were increasing daily.

Early the following morning, preceded by a few horsemen, and carrying rations for only two days, Rowlands led the column out of the camp '… for duty uncertain and full of risk'. The column consisted of eight European officers, 275 natives (mostly Swazis) and some volunteer horsemen. From the mission station the road lay through a deep valley from which, after an ascent of about 200 feet, it opened out into a wide grassy plain, about ten miles in length. To the left of the column, on the distant hills, a number of Zulus could be seen tending to their sheep and cattle. After fording the Inpongo river, a short halt was called before the final advance on the kraal began. From this point onwards the road became more difficult and great caution was taken to prevent the column being ambushed. Two abandoned camps were found where the fires still smoked and, as the column drew near to the kraal, a village was spotted up ahead and the Swazis rushed forward to investigate. Two shots were fired from the huts and some assegais thrown which wounded some of the attacking party but which did not halt their charge. The village was captured and the force carried on to take the kraal at the first rush. Although this action was regarded as a minor one, it did have a number of long term effects in that it boosted the morale of the regular troops, volunteers and Swazis and also re-opened the road from Luneburg to Wood's headquarters at Kambula.

A few days later, Rowlands led another small force out of Luneburg to complete the work begun by Buller against Manyanyoba's stronghold at Eloya mountain. On reaching their objective however, they discovered that the Zulus had gone and they returned, empty handed, to Luneburg.

At the end of February, Rowlands and his staff, received orders to move with all possible haste, to Pretoria and there to take over the command of the garrison as the situation between the British and the Boers had deteriorated. He was to leave five companies of the 80th Regiment at Luneburg and the few irregular mounted forces which he still had under his command were to be sent to Wood. The orders were, for once, clear enough and it was evident that although he was to continue as Commandant of the Transvaal, he was being passed over in favour of Wood as regards the second invasion of Zululand which was then in preparation. Shepstone wrote to him on 25 February:

> I am sure you will not mind my saying this but it is very evident that if you lose your mounted force you will be reduced to the necessity of remaining stationary and your position as Commandant of the Transvaal will be neutralised.

Captain Clarke also wrote: 'Colonel Rowlands feels very much his command being jumped piecemeal by Colonel Wood.' Chelmsford's attitude towards Rowlands became absolutely clear in letters which he wrote to Wood at this time:

> I hope that by this time you have got rid of Rowlands and have got his troops [which] will be a good addition to your force.

and,

> One line to congratulate you on getting rid of Rowlands.

Rowlands was being beaten from his command by underhand methods. He had twice honourably offered to resign his position if he was found to be lacking in the execution of his duties. Twice he had been dissuaded from taking such action by the very persons who, amongst themselves, openly declared their wish to be rid of him. If Chelmsford felt that Rowlands was such a failure as an independent commander then it was his duty to replace him straight away. The fact that the general felt this way and took the action which he did raises a serious question as to his ability as a GOC of troops in the field. Did he in fact lack the moral courage to remove Rowlands or did he feel that by doing so he might open an investigation into his own conduct of the affairs or was it merely a charitable act to save the career of a fellow officer? In view of the manner in which Chelmsford and Wood went about undermining Rowlands' authority, it is of little wonder that the Colonel appeared indecisive. Whichever way he turned, he seemed to come up against opposition from remote sources. Throughout this trying period, Rowlands' one constant source of support was Sir Theophilus Shepstone and even he was about to be removed from his position in the Transvaal.

Shortly before leaving Pretoria, Shepstone wrote to Sir Bartle Frere expressing his concern about a crisis which seemed to be developing in the region.

> Sir Th[eophilus] Shepstone has reason to believe that an understanding exists between the Boer leaders and Cetywayo; and in this state of things recommends the withdrawal of the troops in Sekukuni's Country to Pretoria.

Shepstone had heard rumours that the Zulus were entering the Transvaal and meeting secretly with the Boer leaders who had been expressing their discontent with the British since the annexation of the Transvaal. He feared that this was the prelude to an armed rebellion by the Boers, possibly assisted by the Zulus. Frere contacted Chelmsford and the latter issued the order sending Rowlands back to Pretoria to take command of the forces there in case the situation developed further. Chelmsford had, at last, succeeded in getting Rowlands away from the conflict in Zululand but, in doing so, had placed him in a situation in which he was to earn great credit and restore much of his damaged prestige.

Shepstone's suggestion that Rowlands should assume command in Pretoria and leave the north eastern Transvaal unguarded had been a devious one:

> This would give the Boers to the north east of Pretoria something to do and to think and talk about other than the subversion of the Government.

They would have to protect themselves, which they were well able to do, against any raids that the Basutos may make upon them; although they are given to assume that the hostility of Sikukuni [*sic*] is against the British and not against them; and should their assumption be right the withdrawal of the force which I propose would produce no inconvenience to them.[17]

Chapter 12
Pretoria

Rowlands left Luneburg towards the end of February and, by the time he had arrived in Pretoria, Shepstone had gone, having been replaced by Colonel Owen Lanyon. This new partnership then set about assessing the deeply rooted problems which faced them.

When, in 1877, Shepstone had decided that it would be in the best interest of the British authorities in Cape Colony and Natal to annex the independent Boer territory of the Transvaal (following the discovery of diamonds in the region), the Boers had, quite naturally, objected. Shepstone had then massed infantry and artillery on the Natal-Transvaal border and had even threatened to unleash a Zulu army against them if they refused to comply with his demands. The Boers, still protesting, but able to do little else, were annexed and Shepstone used the abortive Boer expedition against Sekhukhune to illustrate the futility of the continuation of the Transvaal as an independent republic. In 1877, two Boer leaders were sent to London to petition the British Government on behalf of the now defunct republic but met with little sympathy and even less success. The following year a further two Boers were despatched to London (Paul Kruger and Piet Joubert) but met with the same result and, on their return, decided to petition Sir Bartle Frere who was due to visit Pretoria. News of this spread to other Boers who were disaffected with the situation in the Transvaal and they too made their way to the capital to hear what Frere had to say. The events in Zululand in January and February 1879, however, delayed Frere's arrival by a month and the gathering of large numbers of Boers outside Pretoria caused a great deal of concern amongst the authorities. It was this situation that Rowlands faced when he returned to the capital in March.

Having made an assessment of the situation, Rowlands made his report to the Governor's Office in Durban in which he stated that five thousand well armed Boers had assembled on the High Veldt, some

The outskirts of Pretoria, 1879.

fifteen miles outside Pretoria, and were posing a serious military threat to the town as they were behaving in a very violent manner towards the authorities. After completing his detailed inspection of the forces available to him, Rowlands set about preparing the town to repel any attack which the Boers might make. On 18 March, he had reviewed all the Imperial troops and the local volunteers which together numbered about five hundred men.

On 24 March, Lanyon and Rowlands met a deputation from the Boers at Strydon's Farm which was some distance outside Pretoria. Among the group were Joubert, Kruger and Pretorius all of whom demanded independence for the Transvaal and insisted that their demand be presented to Frere when he arrived. They also stated that it was their intention to form three columns which would stop all communications and prevent all supplies either entering or leaving the capital. It was evident that rebellion was in their minds and, unless great care was taken by the British authorities, the situation would deteriorate into open conflict.

Rowlands divided up the limited forces which he had under his command and placed them in positions which he felt would be the most effective in the event of a Boer attack. Barricades were set up in the streets and all major buildings were placed in a defensive state. Mustering places were arranged in the event of a surprise attack and '… every respectable white inhabitant has, upon application, been provided with a good breech loading rifle and 50 rounds of ammunition'.

Early in April, Sir Bartle Frere arrived in Pretoria to assess the situation for himself and to try and find a peaceful solution to the crisis. After examining the defences he wrote to Chelmsford:

> The Barracks, the Church, the Gaol and other places are laagered and fortified and Lanyon and Rowlands agree that the whole of the malcontents would find it difficult to carry or hold the town after mastering its defences.

> This officer [Rowlands] has at his disposal to cover the town and defend the stores, Treasury, Government Offices etc, only two full companies of infantry, no regular cavalry or artillery, two Krupp guns with 25 rounds of ammunition each, 28 rockets with two tubes that he has manufactured on the spot. By careful retrenching he has made the barracks safe against a coup de main as long as the water, which comes from without, was not cut off and by laagering some of the most defensible buildings he felt he could secure the town from occupation with the aid of about 600 efficient volunteers of all sorts.

Frere had several meetings with the Boers and discovered that they had only been prevented from attacking the town by '… the firm attitude and defensive preparations of H.E. the Administrator and of the Commandant.' Despite this, Frere pointed out to Chelmsford that there was a violent minority itching to launch an assault on Pretoria irrespective of the defences. He described the Boers as being well armed, mostly mounted, accustomed to guerrilla warfare and so posted that '… without artillery and cavalry it would have been a bold man who would have undertaken to disperse them with a force six times as large as that at the disposal of Colonel Rowlands.'

Lanyon and Frere impressed upon the Boers the uselessness of their defiant attitude and finally, just when it appeared that the talks were making no headway, the malcontents began to disperse following Frere's promise that he would send a written representation (which the Boers had drawn up) to the government in London. The break up of the Boer force was also caused by many of their number becoming bored with the lack of any action and others losing faith in their leaders. Before leaving, they heard that the British had issued a statement declaring that they were against the annexation of Zululand and demanded that the same statement should apply to the Transvaal and reminded Frere that '... their dispersion was only temporary and that they would probably meet again when sufficient time had elapsed for an answer to their memorial.' Frere and Lanyon informed the Boer leaders that no more armed meetings would be allowed and, whilst agreeing to any discussion which they might ask for, they, as representatives of the British government, would not allow themselves to be intimidated by armed men who threatened force unless their demands were met.

Although the immediate danger had been averted, Rowlands realised that, if Frere and Lanyon were not to be seen as weak, reinforcements would have to be sent to Pretoria and a request was made for a force of '... not less than a wing of a regiment with some cavalry and 2 guns, prepared to act, if necessary, after the next month in order to prevent or disperse any attempt at a renewal of any agitation in camps of armed men.'

With the removal of the immediate threat of the Boers, the problem of Sekhukhune again raised its head. Rowlands and Frere appear to have discussed the Pedi chieftain at some length and reached the conclusion that some sort of action would have to be taken against him as, since the abortive expedition of the previous year, he was still posing a threat to the north-eastern frontier of the Transvaal. Naturally, Rowlands hoped to be given the command of any future assault on the stronghold in the Lulu mountains and thereby make amends for his failure in 1878. Both he and Clarke keenly advocated action adding that if any move were to be made it would have to be done soon and certainly no later than the first week of June. Although the drought of 1878 had been unprecedented, Rowlands did not intend taking the chance of being caught without water for a second time. In order that Chelmsford might see an attack against Sekhukhune as part of an overall campaign against Cetshwayo, Rowlands pointed out that the advance into Zululand could result in large numbers of Zulus fleeing into Sekhukhune's territory and he quoted a letter which he had received from Captain Clarke on 9 April:

> Messages are constantly passing between the natives, both hostile and friendly, urging coalition, and with communications kept up by Cetewayo [sic] and Sekukuni [sic], some combined movement may be reasonably expected. It is probable that a portion of the Zulus will seek protection under

a chief with whom their leader has connection and whose strongholds are believed by the natives to be impregnable. The road between Zululand and Sekukuni's country is open and we have no power to check any movement between the places.

He suggested that a flying column be established to patrol between the Crocodile and Komati rivers and particularly asked, if they were available, for the return of Raaff's Horse and the Border Horse. In addition, he requested four 7lb mountain guns with crews and ammunition, two rocket troughs with Hall 9lb war rockets, two full regiments of infantry, seven hundred mounted volunteers and three thousand natives, preferably Swazis. This suggested force was a considerable increase on that with which he had attempted to subdue the Pedi in 1878.

Rowlands proposed to divide the force into three columns, two of which were to be based at Fort Weeber and Lydenburg while the third, which would be mounted, would clear the northern side of the Oliphant river of all cattle and then assemble at Murder Kopjie. The largest column, based at Fort Weeber, would then advance by way of the Panama valley to the summit of the Lulu range until it was about ten miles from Sekhukhune's Town. At the same time, the Lydenburg column would advance through the Waterfall valley until it reached beyond Sekhukhune's Staadt where it would entrench itself and await developments.

Once the force was in position, the mounted column would sever all communication between the Lulu mountains and the north and cut off Sekhukhune's cattle supply. The other two columns would then move on Sekhukhune's Town from two sides whilst, at the same time, control all access from the south.

The plan was approved by Frere and presented by him to Chelmsford who, somewhat surprisingly, agreed to its implementation. The General promised to send the required reinforcements and instructed Rowlands to proceed with his preparations. By agreeing to this Chelmsford was all but admitting that the force used in 1878 had been far too small to be effective. He wrote to Frere on 21 April:

> I have telegraphed Evelyn Wood that he must manage, if possible, to send two companies of the 80th Regiment and two guns to Standerton, at which place they will be at the disposal of Colonel Rowlands to move wherever he

pleases. I wish I could spare more troops at this juncture for Pretoria as I feel it would facilitate the arrangements in the Transvaal.

Once again, this letter illustrates Chelmsford's ambiguous style of command. He states that Wood must manage '… if possible' to send troops to Rowlands. By implication, therefore, Wood was not compelled to send any troops. The remainder of the force which Rowlands required would have to be raised from volunteers within the Transvaal itself. Lanyon wrote on 26 April:

> I am trying all I can to get a force for Rowlands, as he must be ready to commence work on the 1 June and if we fail in bringing Sekukuni [*sic*] in during the ensuing four months we shall have every native against us up to the Zambezi.

By May, preparations were well advanced and, at the end of the first week, Lanyon wrote:

> I am hard at work getting natives for Rowlands' column and I am going to Sekukuni's mountain with him in order that he may have every assistance the civil power can give him.

Frere however, despite supporting Rowlands' scheme, had misgivings about his ability to command the column. Indeed, he had supported Chelmsford's earlier actions despite, at the time, never having met or dealt with Rowlands. In a letter to the general he wrote:

> I do not know how you will be off for Major-Generals or whether you contemplate sending any of them up here, but Rowlands evidently works best when he has someone to rely on to tell him what to do. He will then do it well. He is as brave as a lion — and full of resource, but he is a man who likes to see his line of duty clearly chalked out for him and not to have to make plans for himself.

In the post-script to the above letter, Frere added 'Both Rowlands and Clarke have an immense amount of information about the eastern districts so that it would be a great misfortune if any one who came would pooh-pooh their experience and set them aside'. Whether this letter influenced Chelmsford or whether Wood had intervened or perhaps the General himself was having second thoughts, it transpired that during the second week of May he wrote to Pretoria ordering a halt to all preparations for the assault on Sekhukhune. Both Rowlands and Lanyon were shocked and the latter wrote to Chelmsford on 14 May:

British Residency, Pretoria, April 1879. Seated outside are [L–R]: Captain Frederick Carrington, Colonel Owen Lanyon, Sir Bartle Frere and Colonel Hugh Rowlands.

If nothing should turn up to prevent me, I propose starting by post-cart on Saturday with Rowlands to join you, for I think it is absolutely necessary that you should hear from us the position of affairs here. The effect of leaving Sekukuni [*sic*] alone for another year will be very serious both as to expenditure and results so I hope we may be able to do something after consulting with you.

Lanyon and Rowlands met Chelmsford on 21 May and consulted and argued with him throughout the day. The General would not be moved on his decision but, in order to placate Rowlands, he offered him a new post as a brigadier-general commanding a brigade on the Lower Tugela river under the command of Major-General Crealock. The rank of brigadier-general would be a local one and would have to be relinquished after the campaign was over. This appointment however, did not mean that Chelmsford had changed his mind about Rowlands' abilities; the promotion was a means of finally removing him from an independent command and placing him under the control of another, proven, officer. This attitude towards Rowlands was clearly reflected in a letter which he wrote to Wood later that same day:

> I have offered Rowlands Pearson's Brigade. In case of acceptance Lanyon will command troops in Transvaal as a temporary measure … and I told him [Lanyon] that with Carrington and Clarke as Lieutenants he would get on much better against Sekukuni [*sic*] than if Rowlands retained the management of affairs.

Rowlands must have realised what was happening and was probably aware that if he remained in the Transvaal any opportunity for an active, combat command would disappear. There was only one way to prove himself to the General and thereby salvage his undoubtedly damaged career; he had to accept the offer of the brigade on the Lower Tugela river. The following day he informed the Chelmsford of his decision but added the proviso that, after the campaign in Zululand was over, and active operations were resumed against Sekhukhune, that he be given some form of command in the force that was employed.

On 26 May, Brigadier-General Hugh Rowlands, accompanied by Captain Harvey, left the Transvaal by post-cart and, after an uneventful journey, reached Major-General Crealock's column on the Lower Tugela on 7 June. There he was given the command of the 1st Brigade and Harvey was appointed his Acting Brigade Major. On 19 June, after nearly two weeks the Brigade left the Tugela river and headed for Fort Crealock where they were to be stationed until the invasion of Zululand began. Here Rowlands was given the responsibility for maintaining the lines of communication in the area as well as the construction of a new fort (Fort Durnford) near the mouth of the Umlalasi river, where supplies could be landed from ships anchored off the coast. Crealock very soon gained a very different opinion to the General as regarding Rowlands' abilities:

> The regular communications along the line of advanced forts viz Crealock, Chelmsford, Tenedos and Pearson … were placed in the charge of one of the best men there, namely Colonel Hugh Rowlands … whose eye for the country, tact and temper with the natives and incessant vigilance eminently qualified him for such a responsibility.

High praise indeed for a man who, in his last command, had received nothing but criticism.

On 27 June, having been joined by Major-General Crealock himself, the column advanced a further four miles and, the following day set up camp about a mile from the coast where they were joined by the remainder of the Division. On 2 July, work began on the construction of a further fort (Fort Richards) between the camp and the sea.

Chelmsford's plan for the second invasion of Zululand rested heavily on Crealock's Division and it was his intention to reward it for its services in the campaign by placing it in the vanguard of the final advance on the Zulu capital at Ulundi. Excitement at the prospect of action mounted among the officers and men but it was not to be. Once more, the force commanded by Rowlands was to be relegated to a backwater for, healthy as the coastal area appeared to be, 'coast sickness' broke out amongst the transport animals which played havoc with the entire division. So bad did the situation become that Crealock was forced to withdraw the 1st Division from its place in the planned invasion and the final honours at Ulundi, on 4 July, fell to the 2nd Division.

On 5 July, before news of the victory at Ulundi had reached the troops of the 1st Division, some seven hundred Zulus with all their cattle, women and children were seen approaching the camp at Fort Richards where they intended to tender their submission and claim the protection of the British Crown. Crealock ordered the full division to parade at mid-day and, at 12.30*p.m.*, he and his staff rode onto the parade ground. The Zulus were then called forward and lay down their arms; the Zulu War, relatively brief in duration but disastrous in its execution, was over.

By this time, Chelmsford had lost his command. After the disaster at Isandhlwana his credibility as a commander had been brought into question and he was replaced by Sir Garnet Wolseley, the founder of the 'Wolseley Ring' in which Wood and Buller were prominent. Rowlands must have taken some pleasure at Chelmsford's downfall but it was doubtful whether the new General Officer Commanding would bring about any improvement in his situation. Chelmsford's departure had been deferred until July, because of the delay in the arrival of Wolseley and the victory at Ulundi was achieved just in time to enable him to salvage some of his reputation. When the General did leave, so did a number of other officers who were his supporters, including Major-General Crealock who, before departing made out a report on the men under his command. Of Rowlands he wrote:

Brigadier General Pearson was succeeded by Col Rowlands, CB, VC, who has given me every assistance since he has been in my command. In his desire to see service with the 1st Division he gave up an independent command in the Transvaal and joined me at the Tugela.

On 11 July, Rowlands left the coast and took command of Fort Chelmsford where he remained until late August when he embarked aboard the transport ship *Egypt* arriving in Portsmouth on 13 October, 1879. Once again, the warrior was returning to Caernarfon and his activities in Africa had not gone unnoticed by the inhabitants of the area. On 26 July, the *Carnarvon & Denbigh Herald* carried the following report:

> The most stirring events of the present campaign in South Africa have taken place outside the district whose safety Colonel Rowlands has had in his charge. He has, however, done a deal of important and good work, although we hear less of it than the operations in Zululand. The Colonel appears to have fully justified Lord Chelmsford's recorded opinion that he was an officer that in whose intelligence and ability his Lordship had every confidence.

Rowlands' fall from grace with Chelmsford had evidently not reached the ears of north Wales!

His impending arrival home was, as in 1856, reported in the local press so that when the train pulled into Bangor Station there was an enthusiastic crowd there to greet him. The same occurred at Port Dinorwic and Griffith's Crossing near Caernarfon. The scenes at Caernarfon Station resembled those of twenty-five years earlier as crowds of people lined the platform to greet him and cheer as he and Mrs Rowlands appeared at the carriage door '... so anxious was each person to see him that it was with difficulty that he managed to reach his carriage outside the station platform'. From the carriage he made a short speech before heading home to Plastirion.

His return to Caernarfon coincided with the preparations for the 1880 National Eisteddfod of Wales which was to be held in the town the following year. A few days after his arrival he attended the Proclamation Ceremony for the Eisteddfod and his entry onto the platform was hailed with great enthusiasm from the crowd which rose to its feet to greet him, cheering loudly and waving hats and pocket handkerchiefs in the air. When the band struck up *Hail the Conquering Hero Comes* the audience again rose to its feet cheering loudly and it was some considerable time before he was able to address the crowd:

The reception which I obtained from you on the Monday evening that I arrived was quite unexpected by me and certainly the enthusiastic reception you have so kindly given me this day has been even more unexpected than the other. I have been away now for over twenty months in South Africa where, for some months, I was comparatively unemployed. I had to go to that country to seek information for the government. I was where not many troops were stationed and nothing much could be done. As one cannot make bricks without straw I applied to Lord Chelmsford to support the volunteer troops I had collected in the year - about eight or nine hundred men. This he declined to do. I then took command of a Brigade under General Crealock which, unfortunately, as you will see in the papers did nothing. I assure you that it is a matter of painful regret to me that I have not been more actively employed during my time of absence. I went to South Africa and sought service there but, unfortunately, it would not come, and now that I have returned home I naturally feel proud that the people of this country, at all events, consider that I have done my part, however humble it may be in the great sphere of action which was open to many in that country. Whenever I am called upon, you may rely on it that I am always ready, I trust I always shall be, as there is some kick in me and, if an opportunity occurs, I hope I shall be more deserving of the favour you have always shown me since I have been a soldier.

This was the speech of an embarrassed and rather bitter man. His feelings about his treatment in Africa can be clearly read between the lines and, as a result of it, he later wrote to the *Carnarvon & Denbigh Herald*:

I shall be much obliged by your correcting in your next impression the statement which I inadvertently made, in an unpremeditated speech ... on 24th of last month, in perusing the account of which I observe that I said that the lower column in which I for time commanded the 1st Brigade under General Crealock 'Did nothing'. I feel it would be most unjust to that column to allow the remark to remain uncontradicted. I therefore take the earliest opportunity of retracting it. The lower column, although not fortunate enough to be up at Ulundi, nevertheless did its part in the operations in Zululand under trying circumstances, in an extremely unhealthy locality, and I should be sorry if any words of mine should have given rise to the impression that such was not the case.

There can be little doubt that his period of service in southern Africa was the most disastrous of Hugh Rowlands' career. How justified the criticisms of him were cannot now be ascertained. He certainly appears to have been hesitant in his actions but whether this was caused by his reaction to the intrigue which was evident or by his own personality cannot be judged. That period of warfare was to prove the downfall of many of the main protagonists and, as will be seen, Rowlands was to emerge from it far less tarnished than most.

Lord Chelmsford spent the latter years of his life very quietly. He never recovered from the disaster at Isandhlwana and, although supported by the Queen and rewarded with honours, he was shunned by the Government, particularly Disraeli. He was promoted to full Lieutenant General in 1882 and General in 1888 but spent several years on half-pay and was never again given the command of a force in the field. He died suddenly in 1905, in the middle of a game of billiards at his London club.

Sir Bartle Frere became the subject of a bitter campaign orchestrated by Gladstone in 1880. He refused to resign his post even when his salary was cut and was eventually recalled from Cape Town. He died four years later, discredited and in debt, trying to defend his actions to a public that had no interest in listening to him.

Evelyn Wood remained in South Africa and served in an administrative post in the Boer War of 1881 and, the following year, served in a similar capacity in Egypt. Despite all his successes in Zululand he never again command troops in battle, his career continuing in a series of important administrative posts. He died in 1919 with the rank of Field Marshal.

Redvers Buller's career continued until the end of the century when, as a Lieutenant-General, he commanded the Imperial forces in the opening stages of the second Boer War. In that capacity he proved to be a disaster as witness the horrific tale of blunders during the Battle of Spion Kop. He was then placed under the command of Lord Roberts and, after refusing to resign, retired from the army on half-pay in 1901. He died in 1908.

Among the few officers who received recognition for their service in Zululand and Transvaal was Hugh Rowlands who was granted the Reward for Distinguished Service. From being among enemies in Africa, he seems to have been surrounded by friends and supporters in Britain, not the least of which was the celebrated journal *The Army & Navy Gazette* which reported:

> We are glad to hear that Colonel Hugh Rowlands, VC, CB, has been noted for a distinguished service award. Colonel Rowlands richly deserves this recognition, for he has been serving, uninterruptedly, at the Cape for close on

two years; he has passed through two campaigns there, and has already completed thirty years service — which is considered to qualify for the pension.

The same publication later added:

It has been definitely decided that Sir Evelyn Wood shall not have the rank of Major General conferred upon him, as it is contended, and with some reason, that Sir Evelyn could on no grounds of equity or justice be elevated to Generals rank over the heads of such men as Colonels F C Hassard, CB, Hugh Rowlands, VC, CB ... all of whom have been serving at the Cape during recent hostilities, and are held to have equal claims to the favourable consideration of Her Majesty.

On 13 December, *The Army & Navy Gazette* declared that Hugh Rowlands ought to be considered for the award of the Order of St Michael and St George which was bestowed upon those persons, both civil and military, who had rendered a special service to a British colony. Later the same month, Rowlands was one of the officers who had served in Zululand who were invited to a dinner, given in their honour, at Windsor Castle.

Chapter 13
General Officer

Hugh Rowlands, having reverted to the rank of Colonel on leaving the Cape, was now unemployed and on half-pay as he was not attached to any particular regiment. In July 1880, he was appointed Assistant Adjutant and Quarter-Master General for the North British District in Edinburgh where his duties involved assisting the Adjutant to the GOC in the day-to-day running of the command as well as being responsible for the movement, billeting and quartering of the troops and for all matters relating to barracks, hospitals, canteens, lighting, fuel, cooking, etc. Although an important position, it was not the type of post that he would have found particularly satisfying for any great length of time. Consequently, within a few months he was once again en-route to India with the rank of Brigadier-General to take over the command of the Peshawar Brigade in the Punjab. This was an important posting as Peshawar was the north-west frontier station of the Indian Empire, the town which guarded the border with Afghanistan and situated only ten miles from the famed Khyber Pass. It was a posting that was much sought after by officers as the opportunities for active service on the north-west frontier were good due to the turbulent Afghan tribesmen who populated the mountains. An active command was, however, denied to him once again as, having been promoted to Major-General in July 1881, he returned to Britain in August 1882 to take over the command of the 3rd Infantry Brigade at Aldershot. These two prestigious commands, coming shortly after each other would seem to indicate that he had overcome the problems of 1878–9 and that his conflict with Lord Chelmsford was a thing of the past.

In 1880, General Sir Frederick Roberts, VC, had been appointed Commander-in-Chief of the Madras Presidency Army in India. It was his ambition to eventually command the whole Indian Army and to join together the three Presidency Armies of Madras, Bengal and Bombay into one force. To achieve this he believed that the quality and capability of the three forces would have to be brought up to the same standard of efficiency. Roberts saw his appointment as C-in-C Madras as an opportunity to make a start on his plans for redevelopment and, shortly after taking up his post, he reviewed his command:

> I made long tours in order to acquaint myself with the needs and capabilities of the Madras Army. I tried hard to discover in them those fighting qualities which had distinguished their forefathers ... But long years of peace and security and prosperity ... had upon them ... a softening and deteriorating effect; and I was forced to the conclusion that the ancient military spirit had died in them ... and that they could no longer with safety be pitted against warlike races or employed outside the limits of southern India.

He later wrote:

> From the time I became Commander-in-Chief Madras, until I left India, the question of how to render the army ... as perfect a fighting machine as possible ... caused me most anxious thought. The first step was to substitute men of the more warlike and hardy races. It became essential to have in our native army men who might confidently be trusted to take their share of the fighting against a European foe.

In the British Army the superiority of one regiment over another was largely a matter of training and leadership. Roberts realised that the same was not true in India but felt that a great deal could be done to improve the situation by improving the leadership. He substantiated this view by citing as an example the Madras Sappers, who were led by officers seconded from the Royal Engineers, men who had volunteered because they were keen to advance their careers. Having taken over the command of the Sappers they were anxious to make their reputations by creating efficiency in their men. The Madras infantry and cavalry on the other hand were of poor quality and were commanded by European officers who had joined them for life. These officers had few career prospects, there was no fixed time scale for promotion and little chance of seeing any active service. This, felt Roberts, led to slackness and inefficiency and he saw his main course of action as being that of trying to revitalise the Madras Army. He needed new blood for the officer corps and outlined what he saw as the two main criteria for their selection:

> 1. The appointment of generals to high commands in India are, I believe, greatly determined by the authorities at home. It is most desirable that

Two views of Bangalore. Above, the Cubbou Park and below, the Lal Bagh.

officers should not be placed in positions of responsibility in India who have little or no acquaintance with the country, unless under very special circumstances. No officer of the British Service can be appointed to the brigade staff in India, who has been absent from the country for more than seven years.

2. I am strongly of the opinion that no one should get a command in peace unless he is considered fit to command in war. Fitness for war should be the test; anyone who could not be trusted in war should be passed over, so far as appointments in India are concerned.

Hugh Rowlands certainly qualified for an Indian command under the first category outlined by Roberts. Indeed, Rowlands' arch-rival in South Africa, Evelyn Wood and Sir Garnet Wolseley were specially noted by Roberts as being unqualified under this category. Rowlands' suitability under the second category, however, can be doubted. If Lord Chelmsford's opinion of him was correct he was not suitable for a command in war; as a second-in-command he might be successful but, with the rank of Major-General, should a war come he would almost certainly be given an independent active service command. The outcome of this situation finally put an end to any speculation which might still have existed about Rowlands' capabilities. On 21 April 1884, Major-General Rowlands was appointed to the command of the Bangalore Division of the Madras Army, under the direct command of General Roberts who wrote, regarding the appointment, to HRH the Duke of Cambridge, Commander-in Chief of the British Army.

> General Payne informs me that he has heard by telegraph ... that he is to be succeeded by Major-General Rowlands ... I believe the officer Your Royal Highness has selected is, in every way, admirably suited for the command.

Two months later, after forming a clearer view of Rowlands, Roberts noted:

> I think General Rowlands an excellent appointment; he has the credit of being an energetic, able officer, and will no doubt do well at Bangalore.

Bangalore was regarded by many, including Roberts, as the finest command in India with the possible exception of Rawlpindi. Cornet Whale of the 15th Hussars had written of it in the 1840s:

> Never shall I forget the sunshine and fruit and flowers, and cool verandahs and beautiful bathrooms and luxurious bedrooms, and white robed

Above: Major General Rowlands, VC, CB, and his staff at a march-past of the Bangalore Division, Madras Army, 22 December 1888.

Below: March-past of the Bangalore Division, Madras Army, Mont Uli, December 1887.

attendants, and horses, and dogs, and guns, the well furnished libraries. Oriental life in those days was truly delightful ──no hurry and scurry but plenty of time, servants and money.

Despite the passage of forty years and the Indian Mutiny, little had changed in Bangalore by the time Hugh Rowlands assumed his command in April 1884. Duties for British officers were few and mostly carried out in the morning before the temperature got too high. Many officers had their wives and families with them and the social life was plentiful, with a leave period of up to sixty days a year during which time officers could do more or less as they wished. Those who sought European society with hotels, theatres, dances and similar social functions, would go to a hill station, the most popular in Madras being Ootacamund, where the cooler temperature allowed them to escape the heat of the plains and enjoy a more active life. Dinner parties, dances and theatricals were a nightly occurrence and in the afternoons there were race-meetings, polo tournaments, dog shows etc without end. Stupid gossip or shop replaced intelligent conversation. There was such extravagance that many of the officials were either in debt or could just scrape along.

There were also other distractions for leave periods. Big game hunting was always popular and involved not only the skill and excitement of tracking down and stalking a quarry but also journeys into the more remote regions and contact with the unsophisticated mountain people. Mounted sports such as pig-sticking were also popular and jackal-hunting was regarded as a first rate substitute for fox-hunting.

Rowlands appears to have set to his command with his usual vigour and efficiency as an administrator. True to Roberts' wishes, he implemented new training programmes for the Division and exercise camps, a novelty in the past, became regular occurrences. When the machine-gun was first introduced to the sub-continent, it was the Bangalore Division which carried out the first trials. Roberts was impressed with Rowlands both as a commander and as a man but the latter does not appear to have been too happy at Bangalore:

> I am sorry to say that General Rowlands does not care for Bangalore, and he has, he tells me, written to General Whitmore asking to be transferred to Bengal. He is certainly not well, and Mrs Rowlands was also suffering from fever: this added to their being more familiar with the ways and customs of northern India, is probably the reason why General Rowlands wishes for a

change. I shall be sorry to lose him, I like him personally, and he seems to be a thoroughly good officer, but Your Royal Highness will perhaps not object to meeting his wishes.

His wish for a command in Bengal could, once again, be evidence of his desire to see active service before he could be regarded as too old for such duties or it may have been that the heat in Madras was too great.* Whatever his reasons, however, his request was denied and he remained at Bangalore for the remainder of his service in India.

In August 1885, Roberts was appointed Commander-in-Chief of the Bengal Army with supervisory authority over Madras and Bombay. His replacement in Madras was not appointed straight way and Rowlands was given the temporary command of the

A rather frail looking Hugh Rowlands, photograph taken in Madras, c.1886.

Madras Army as Provincial Commander-in-Chief whilst handing over command of Bangalore to his second-in-command. He was too far down the seniority list to be given the permanent command of Madras as the post carried with it the rank of Lieutenant General. On 1 March 1886, Lieutenant General Sir Herbert Macpherson, VC, arrived to take over the Madras command and Rowlands reverted to being GOC of the Bangalore Division. Shortly afterwards, Macpherson was given

---

* If Hugh Rowlands had been infected with malaria during his service in the West Indies in the 1850s, then it is likely that the illness would recur, particularly if he served in the climate that prevailed in Madras. He was less likely to suffer from malaria were he to serve in northern India.

command of an expedition in Burma where he contracted a fever and died in October 1886 as a result of which, Rowlands was, once again, given temporary command of the Presidency Army.

In 1888, it was decided that Bangalore, until that time categorised as a First Class District, should become a Second Class District which only warranted a Brigade Command. As Hugh Rowlands' period of command was due to end the following year it was decided that the change in status of the district would take place at the same time. The remaining months of his tour of duty passed peacefully and on 20 April 1889 he handed over the command to Brigadier-General Bengough on which occasion the local press commented:

> Our retiring General has often acted as Commander in Chief of the Madras Army, and strong and healthy as he is, we have every hope that he is still destined to find some high and important position in the army. He and Mrs Rowlands have always been popular members of society in Bangalore. He is a strict disciplinarian, though in many cases, in confirming courts martial, he has leaned on the side of mercy. General Rowlands, we have no doubt, will look back upon the period of his command of the Mysore District with none but pleasant feelings and we wish him and his family every prosperity.

On 22 April, he embarked aboard the SS *Clan Macarthur* bound for London. This was to be the last time that he sailed from India after a total of nearly a quarter of a century of service in the sub-continent. On his arrival in Britain some three weeks later he was listed as an unattached general officer. He did not receive a new command, although remaining on full pay, and much of his time was spent at Plastirion with his growing family. On New Year's Day, 1890, he was promoted to Lieutenant General but it was not until 21 June 1893, that he was given any military duties. On that date he was appointed Lieutenant of the Tower of London, one of the oldest posts in the personal award of the monarch. It was a post which, by tradition, was given to a high ranking army officer as a reward for his services. Officially, the Lieutenant was responsible for the guarding of all prisoners held in that building but, by the 1890s this duty had become very rare indeed and the post was more a title of honour which carried with it accommodation in the Tower.

Rowlands returned to full time military duties on 5 January 1894 when he was appointed to the command of the Scottish District with his headquarters in Edinburgh Castle. Ten months later, on 16 October, he

Lt. General Hugh Rowlands, VC, CB, in the uniform of Lieutenant of the Tower of London, 1893. Note the emblem of the White Tower on his collar.

was promoted to the rank of General. He remained in the Scottish Command until 6 May 1896, when he retired from the army having reached the maximum age for a soldier of his rank. Rowlands, however, had made an error with his date of birth many years previously and, consequently, he was in fact one year over the maximum age allowed for an officer of his rank.

Chapter 14
Retirement

With his active military career over, Hugh Rowlands could look forward to the life a country gentleman and consider that, despite the obstacles that he had encountered on the way, he had reached the top of the military ladder; only the rank of Field Marshal had eluded him. As a junior officer, regimental commander and general officer he had been popular and respected by most of those whom he had served with. His personal courage had earned him the Victoria Cross which, even today, is the most coveted decoration for gallantry. He had always shown a concern for those under his command but, when it was necessary, he had not been afraid of casualties. He did, however, refuse to needlessly sacrifice men's lives.

At the time of his retirement he was three months short of completing forty-seven years service — the longest serving officer of the nineteenth century, Field Marshal Lord Roberts, managed to reach the half-century but he had started his career at the age of fifteen.

Returning to Plastirion after so many years away must have been a strange sensation. The house and the estate had become his on the death of his mother in 1875 but, for the intervening twenty years, it had stood empty for long periods. He immediately set about carrying out improvements to the estate aimed at making it a successful commercial enterprise. A new house was constructed near the farm-yard and a bailiff employed to run the estate. New stables were built in 1896, waterworks having already been completed five years previously; a house for the estate gardener was built at Glynifor in 1904 and several new farm buildings were constructed. He also built dwellings in the village of Llanrug for his tenants and employees and made considerable additions to his property in the parish of Llanwnda. The main house at Plastirion was enlarged and modernised, and the interior decorated with souvenirs of his career. The decor was decidedly Indian in tone and not to everybody's taste:

Lt. General Hugh Rowlands, VC, CB, in full dress uniform.

The interior of the house was very formal. Alarming really. The drawing room was clutter of Indian things, brass trays, fringy fans ... from Llwyn y brain, our house nearly a mile away, we could hear a donkey, who dragged Mrs R's chair about, letting fly with an ear-shattering bray if it was going to rain, with supporting chorus of screaming peacocks. [The house was] encircled by woods I remember a rookery that speckled the sky with black wheeling dots. In the grounds was a small lake. It was down by the Seiont, picking blackberries, that we came upon General Rowlands fishing. He had got a salmon on his line which was tangled in an over-hanging bough and I waded in and got it ashore for him. He gave me a book on fishing which I kept for a long time, Hoffland's *British Angler's Manual*.

The same author, Berta Ruck, also recalled the image which the retired General gave to the children of the parish:

General Rowlands I remember as a veteran but persistent Dandy of the Old School as he appeared every Sunday in Llanrug Church. He kept his hair and his waxed moustache a rich brown, his waist-line encased in corsets, his feet in tight patent leather boots.

Sternly our father informed us giggle-prone children that:'Any soldier who had won the VC in the Crimean War might be allowed to wear what he chose.

Hugh Rowlands was a regular sight in Llanrug and Caernarfon, wandering along the roads wearing knee britches, ribbed socks carrying

Crimean veterans and officers of the Welch Regiment at Llandaff Cathedral for the laying-up of the regiment's Crimean Colours. Hugh Rowlands is standing seventh from the left. [Welch Regiment Museum]

a stick and accompanied by his small dog. His tall well-built frame was also to be seen astride his favourite horse and the family's love for those animals went so far as to cause them to ban motor vehicles from their estate during the early years of the twentieth century. His presence in the village had a lasting impression on the children who would rush to assist him with the opening of a gate for which duty they would receive a small sum of money. Survivors of that now distant time recall a short verse that they used to sing in the school playground:

> *Beth yw'r cynwrf sydd yn bod?*
> *General Rowlands sydd yn dod*
> *O'r Crimea.*

His pastimes were those of a country gentleman; hunting and fishing in the hills and rivers around Plastirion with his friends Mr Barnard of Bryn Bras Castle and Sir William Preece of Caeathro, the famed telegraphic engineer. Much of his time was also devoted to his duties as a Justice of the Peace, serving as the Chairman of the Caernarfon Bench.

Despite his long years away from Wales, Hugh Rowlands never forgot the language of his ancestors and spoke it whenever the opportunity arose, despite it having become rather rusty. Mr Isaac Lloyd (the poet Glan Rhyddallt) recalled:

> I heard him speaking Welsh, but not fluently, when he was the chairman of the charity committee which met in Glan Moelyn School. When it was over he would ask us — 'Did I speak Welsh well tonight?'— at which point everyone praised him of course.

Another of his great interests was the church and he served for many years as a churchwarden of St Michael's, Llanrug. When a restoration appeal was opened in the early years of the present century, Hugh Rowlands was one of the driving forces and greatest benefactors of the ancient foundation.

He took his role as village squire very seriously and proved, although never a very rich man, to be something of a local philanthropist. Every year, on Whit Monday, local organisations led by a band, marched to Plastirion where they received a meal paid for by the General (at an annual cost of about £100). He donated a free clubhouse to Clwb Glannau Ifor and always gave generously of both his time and his

Hugh Rowlands in retirement, outside the lodge at Plastirion.

General Sir Hugh Rowlands, VC, KCB, *in full dress uniform.*
This photograph, taken shortly after the award of the KCB, shows the
Mameluke scimitar presented to him by the people of Caernarfon in 1856.

Plastirion, Llanrug, the family home of General Sir Hugh Rowlands. This photograph was taken after the completion of various renovations and modernisations in the 1890s.

money to any special event in the village such as the celebrations for the coronation of King Edward VII. On a wider stage he served as Deputy Lieutenant for the County of Caernarfon.

Rowlands was not forgotten by his country after his retirement. On 8 October 1897, he was appointed Colonel of the Duke of Wellington's (West Riding) Regiment and, in the Queen's Birthday Honours List of 1898, he was created a Knight Military Commander of the Order of the Bath.

Retirement did not, however, bring unlimited joy to the old soldier. In 1903, his only son, Hugh Barrow Rowlands, died while serving as a Major in the King's African Rifles. The blow was a crushing one as Sir Hugh explained in a letter to a close friend:

> I write on behalf of Lady R and myself to thank you for your warm letter of condolence with us in our irreparable loss, a loss that can never be replaced in this world. It was very soothing to read your letter as it was replete with sympathy for us in our deep sorrow. It was some consolation that he died in the service of his King and country, and in an eminently distinguished manner, as several who fought in the same fields have testified. Well my dear old friend there is nothing to be done, but to accept it in all humility, the will

General Sir Hugh Rowlands,
VC, KCB, c.1900.

The only known photograph of Lady
Isabella Jane Rowlands, taken at
Plastirion c.1903.

of Him who could never do wrong. Poor young fellow, he had laid a good foundation for a brilliant [career] had his life been spared.

The shock appears to have had an even greater effect upon Lady Rowlands and it seems that she never recovered from the loss of her only son. This put a great strain on life at Plastirion and those that recall the General's latter years praise him for his tolerance and understanding as his wife blamed him for their son's death.

Their only other child also brought problems in the General's declining years when her marriage to Captain Arthur Hume failed and she returned to the family home with her two small daughters. It was perhaps these two small children, Miriam and Marjorie, that brought him the most joy as his life drew towards its close and he certainly had a profound effect upon them.

By 1907, Sir Hugh's health appears to have been deteriorating and his public appearances became fewer. In 1908, whilst staying in Cheltenham he wrote to his solicitor in Caernarfon:

> I still have the rheumatic pains, but the worst thing is my digestion which was completely ruined by Thomas's Poison and I fear that it will be a long time before I am able to take ordinary food.

During the early summer of 1909, he was admitted to the Carnarvon Hospital but was allowed to return home in July. As soon as he felt fit enough to go for a walk, he was reported to have hurried to a high spot which commanded a view of the house at Plastirion where he rested for a while before returning. This was his last recorded excursion as his recovery was only temporary. On Thursday, 29 July 1909, he collapsed at his home and, on Sunday, 1 August he died. The cause of death was given as bronchiectasis, exhaustion and toxaemia.

The funeral was arranged for 5 August when a private service was held in the house after which the cortége made its way to the parish church. The coffin, draped in the Union Flag, was conveyed the half-mile journey on a gun carriage and six non-commissioned officers of the Duke of Wellington's Regiment acted as pall bearers. Inside the church the service was conducted by the Bishop of Bangor and the Curate of Llanrug. The family mourners were all female (the male line having died out with the death of Sir Hugh's only son) and among the crowd gathered at the graveside were the servants of the estate and the tenants, several local dignitaries and a number of officers and men of the Duke of

Left: The grave of General Sir Hugh and Lady Rowlands, St. Michael's churchyard, Llanrug.

Below: The orders, decorations and medals of General Sir Hugh Rowlands, displayed at the Welch Regiment Museum, Cardiff Castle. They are [L–R]: Top — KCB, CB Bottom — VC, Crimea Medal (bars for Alma, Inkerman and Sebastopol); South Africa Medal (bar for 1878-79), Légion d'Honneur, Order of the Medjidie (Turkey), Turkish Crimea Medal.

Wellington's Regiment. Sadly, there was no representative of Sir Hugh's old regiment, the 41st Regiment of Foot. As the coffin was lowered into the grave a volley was fired over it as a final salute to the old soldier. The epitaph on the grave reads simply:

In Sacred Memory of
General Sir Hugh Rowlands, KCB, VC,
of Plastirion
Who Passed to Rest on the First Day of August, 1909
Aged 81 Years
Beloved of His Country Which He Served So Well
And of All Who Knew Him

Eight years later, Lady Isabella Rowlands died at the family's London home in Paddington and her body was brought back to Llanrug and buried beside that of her husband.

Appendix I:
Major Hugh Barrow Rowlands, 1870–1903

Hugh Barrow, the only son of General Sir Hugh and Lady Isabella Rowlands of Plastirion was born at Subathoo, India on 22 January 1870. At the age of nineteen he was commissioned as a 2nd Lieutenant in The Suffolk Regiment, promoted Lieutenant on 5 December 1893 and Captain on 30 July 1898, shortly before he transferring as a Loan Officer to the 2nd Battalion, British Central African Regiment (CAR) with the local rank of Major.

He served with the CAR in the Ashanti War of 1900 where he first saw action as part of the Flying Column commanded by Lieutenant Colonel Brake, which left Kumasi in late August and returned in mid-September after attacking Queen Ashantua's forces at the village of Ojesu, which was destroyed along with many other rebel villages. On 30 September he was present at the action at Bassa.

During a period of leave in 1901, he rejoined the Suffolk Regiment in South Africa where he was actively employed against the Boers in the Transvaal. Whilst there, he served as a signalling officer to a column of mounted infantry which was responsible for holding a line of blockhouses.

On 7 April 1902, he was posted to the King's African Rifles (as the Central African Regiment was now known), which was serving in Somaliland, East Africa. Their duties in that country were to form part of the force trying to destroy the rebels of the 'Mad' Mullah.

In April 1903, he was given command of an infantry column which was part of a force under the command of Major John Gough of the Rifle Brigade. The column was to advance from Bohotle to Danot in two forces, one under the command of Major Gough and the second under the command of Major Rowlands. At 4*p.m.* on 13 April, Gough's column left Bohotle and was followed shortly afterwards by Rowlands' column. Three days later, Gough's men captured two of the enemy who informed

Hugh Barrow Rowlands, only son of General Sir Hugh and Lady Rowlands.

them that three days previously, they had met the 'Mad' Mullah's scouts and been told by them that there was water at Danot but that it was held by the Mullah's mounted riflemen. Gough's column continued the advance, but Captain Rolland, with one of the prisoners, re-turned to the column commanded by Rowlands and informed him that they were to continue the march towards Danot but, if no further orders were received by the following morning, the force was to return to Bohotle.

When Gough's mounted scouts reached Danot they discovered that the supply of water was sufficient for only three days and so, on 17 April, Gough sent orders instructing Rowlands to return to Bohotle. However, when the main column arrived at Danot, they discovered more water than had been expected and a communication was sent to Rowlands countermanding the earlier instructions and telling him to advance and link up with the main force. The orders failed to arrive and on the following morning, Gough received news that Rowlands intended to commence his return to Bohotle on the 19 April at which point he immediately sent fresh orders and, in the early hours of 20 April, Rowlands' column joined the main force having marched 35 miles through dense, dry bush in tremendous heat.

Patrols were sent out to try and locate the enemy and capture some prisoners for interrogation but to no avail. At 4.30*a.m.* on 22 April, Gough ordered the column to march out of Danot and, some three hours later, they were fired upon by some the the Mullah's men. The attack was easily driven off by the Somali Mounted Infantry. At 9.15*a.m.*, Gough received word that the enemy's main force was advancing upon them and he gave orders for defences to be prepared. An hour later the attack commenced on three sides of the British position. Due to the dense bush and long grass firing was at close range (some 20–50 yards) and continued until 2*p.m.* when, with his ammunition starting to run short, Gough ordered a withdrawal towards Danot.

After a lull of only fifteen minutes and before any move could be made, the enemy again attacked. Captains Walker and Townsend led a bayonet charge into the bush which cleared the enemy thus enabling the withdrawal, in the form of a moving square, to begin. At 5.30*p.m.* the rearguard and sides of the square were heavily attacked and the column was halted and two more bayonet charges were made by the King's African Rifles during which Captains Bruce and Godfrey were killed. Inside the square, Major Sharp was wounded. In a letter to his father, General Sir Charles Gough, VC, Major Gough later wrote a description of the events which followed:

> I then kept on walking round, talking to the men and impressing on them to be careful of their ammunition. As I was standing talking to Rowlands and was suggesting his making a charge with his men, a bullet went just past my back and hitting Rowlands through the arm went into the back; he gave a grunt, just as if he was hit in the wind, boxing, and lay down. I turned him over and did what I could for him…and in striking contrast to Sharp who became quite hysterical.

The firing ceased at about 5.45*p.m.* and the force managed to reach Danot at 1.15*a.m.* without further incident. On 28 April, they reached Bohotle and all the wounded were reported to be doing well. In his report Gough stated:

> I cannot speak too highly about the behaviour of all ranks. It could not have been better, the Somalis surprising everyone in their steadiness and dash, the 2nd Battalion K.A.R. having both officers wounded and losing 11 men killed and wounded out of 30, yet full of dash and fight… At some future time I hope to be allowed to bring forward the names of officers and men for the consideration of the AOC.

As a result of this action three officers received the Victoria Cross. Gough nominated Captains Walker and Rolland for the coveted decoration for their gallant efforts attempting to save the life of Captain Bruce. What Gough omitted to mention was his own part in the attempted rescue and subsequently, when the full story emerged, he was also awarded the Victoria Cross, the first time that the award had been given to a father (General Sir Charles Gough), uncle (General Sir Hugh Gough) and son (Major John Gough).

Major Rowlands had survived the remainder of the action and the subsequent withdrawal to Danot and then Bohotle and his condition was described in a letter written by Major Gough:

> Poor old Major Rowlands had his arm (left one luckily) taken off two days ago. I am most awfully sorry, he is such a fine fellow and took all his sufferings so well and cheerfully. He told me that by rights it should have been my arm as I was standing talking to him and had just moved when the bullet went close by my back and hit him. I tried to cheer him up by telling him it was his good looks that had attracted the enemy, but he wouldn't see it in that light.

Rowlands appeared to be on the mend and reports to that effect were sent to his family. Then, he contracted malaria and his condition deteriorated rapidly:

> Since I last wrote poor Major Rowlands has died. I am terribly distressed as he did such good work for me at Danot and was one of the best fellows. He really died of fever as his wounds had almost completely healed up but he could not shake off his fever.

He died on 17 June and was buried at Bohotle. He had, as his father said, laid the foundation of a very promising career. Captain Gordon of the Gordon Highlanders wrote to the General shortly after Major Rowlands' death:

> We were together in the Central African Regiment for over two years and in Ashanti, when owing to Colonel Brake being invalided home the command fell upon me and he was my Adjutant. During that time one thoroughly learnt [of him] as a real friend and a fine soldier. No man deserved more than him in Ashanti and it was awfully hard that he did not get any reward. He was such a fine soldier and so popular with everyone who knew him, whether black or white, and it does seem cruel to have been cut off just as he was getting his opportunity.

General Sir Hugh Rowlands had received remarkably rapid promotion during his early career but his son was advancing even more rapidly. In

Sketch by Melton Prior of Major Gough's square at the battle of Daratoleh, 22 April 1903. Gough is standing (right) speaking with Captain Bruce. Just to the right of him is Horton dressing the wounded Major Hugh Rowlands.

1903, the absence of any direct communication had resulted in Gough's column being unaware that another British force under the command of Colonel Plunket, King's African Rifles, had suffered a severe reverse at the hands of the Mullah's force only a few days previously and that consequently, as the most senior officer of the regiment, Major Hugh Rowlands would have taken over command at the age of thirty-three. John Gough went on to become one of the brightest stars of the British Army and was killed by a German sniper early in the Great War and was awarded a posthumous knighthood. There can be little doubt that Rowlands would also have reached general officer rank by 1914 and he might have played a major role in that horrendous conflict.

His death was reported in the *Army & Navy Gazette:*

> He was the worthy son of a distinguished soldier; devoted to his profession and determined, if possible, to rise in it, as he would have been bound to had he been spared. In him the Suffolk Regiment loses a brave officer who had, throughout his service, set an example to all under him and fully upheld the credit of his cloth. It may be some consolation to his sorrowing parents to know that throughout the Suffolk Regiment their gallant son will be remembered as a good soldier who did his duty cheerfully and well, and died as he would have wished a soldier's death.

In November 1903, the Bishop of Bangor conducted a memorial service to Major Hugh Barrow Rowlands at the parish church in Llanrug and dedicated a memorial plaque and window, given by General Sir Hugh and Lady Rowlands, to his memory. A second plaque was also given by the parishioners of Llanrug and the officers of the Suffolk Regiment.

Appendix II
John 'Jackie' Rowlands, 1873–1900

John (Jackie) Rowlands was born on 23 August 1873 at 22 Grosvenor Street, Chester, the only son of John and Charlotte Rowlands (neé Humphreys) and grandson of John Rowlands of Plastirion, Llanrug. His father, a practising solicitor, was the older brother of General Sir Hugh Rowlands, VC, KCB, of Plastirion.

Jackie was educated at Sutton Valence School, Kent, where he gained a formidable reputation as a sportsman, captaining the 1st XV and representing the school in various field sports. Whilst at the school he was asked to play for Richmond RFC and the London Welsh RFC.

His movements after leaving school in 1893 are not known but, in 1895, he was living in South Africa where he was employed by the Crown Reef Mine on the Rand and played rugby for the Pirates RFC. He returned home to Britain in 1898 and stayed with his mother and sister who, by this time, were living at Mount Pleasant, Llanberis. The following year he returned to South Africa arriving there only three weeks before the outbreak of the second Boer War.

On 17 December 1899, at Port Elizabeth, Jackie Rowlands volunteered for service as a trooper in 2nd Brabant's Horse (Service Number 689), a volunteer cavalry unit. The regiment was commanded by Lieutenant Colonel H. M. Grenfell (late of the Life Guards) and was involved in the famed siege of Wepener when they were attacked for sixteen days by forces under the command of Christian de Wet until relieved by Lord Roberts.

In April 1900, Trooper Rowlands was part of a force which fought at Spitzkop where he was taken prisoner by the Boers. He remained in Boer hands until his release at Pretoria and discharge on 15 October. During his captivity Rowlands, along with numerous others, had been subjected to very poor sanitary conditions and lack of adequate nourishment so that, after his release and move to Durban, he was taken ill with an attack of enteric fever and was admitted to Addlington Hospital where he died on 12 November 1900. He was buried in Grave 7, Block 9 of the Church of England Section, West Street Cemetery, Durban.

A memorial plaque was erected in St Padarn's Church, Llanberis and his name was included on a memorial window at Sutton Valence School.

Appendix III:
Marjorie Hume, 1900–1976

Marjorie Hume was born at Great Yarmouth on 27 January 1900, the daughter of Captain Arthur and Mrs Violet Hume, and grandaughter of General Sir Hugh Rowlands, VC, KCB. Much of her early life was spent at her grandfather's home, Plastirion, Llanrug and Tyddyn Elan, Llanrug. Both she and her sister Miriam decided upon a career in the theatre and it was whilst she was appearing in the production *Maid of the Mountain* that she was spotted by the infant British cinema industry and switched from the stage to the screen. She had already gained notice as an actress in the plays *My Lady's Dress, The Men Who Stayed at Home* and *Milestones* before reaching the age of twenty.

She had a string of screen successes between the wars in both silent and talking films, including: *The Swindler, Scarlet Kiss, Kitty Tailleur, Bluff, A Prince of Lovers, Love and the Whirlwind, Silent Evidence, Simonne Everard, M'Lord of the White Road, Two little Vagabonds, Squire of Long Hadley, King of the Castle, Wonderful Wooing, A Columbo Night, This Marriage Business, Afterwards, Young Woodley, Triumph of the Scarlet Pimpernel, Lord Richmond in the Pantry, Deadlock, Betrayal, Up to the Neck, The Call of Youth, The Keeper of the Door, Lady Tetley's Decree, The Duchess of Seven Dials, The Great Day, The Reaping, A Royal Demand, White Lilac, Cross Currents, Late Extra, Member of the Jury, The Limping Man, Children*

Marjorie Hume, the grandaughter of General Sir Hugh Rowlands.

187

Galore and her last film, released in May, 1957, *The Curse of Frankenstein.*

Marjorie married London stockbroker Eric Lindsay and died at her home in Esher, Surrey in 1976. They had no children.

Appendix IV

Regulation Prices of Commissions, 1821 Warrant

Commissions	Prices*	Difference in Value
Ensign	£ 450	—
Lieutenant	£ 700	£1,100
Captain	£1,800	£1,100
Major	£3,200	£1,400
Lt. Colonel	£4,500	£1,300

•These prices wereofficial but it was common for officers to far sums far in excess of these in order the ensure a commission. Officers did, upon purchasing a higher rank, sell the rank which they were leaving, a transaction which went part of the way towards covering the cost of the promotion. When an officer retired from the service he sold his rank and the money thus raised served as a form of 'lump sum' payment for his retirement.

Real Income derived from a Purchased Commission, 1850

Rank	Pay & Allowances	Interest & Expenses*	Difference
Lt. Colonel	£365-0-0	£380-12-11	-£15-12-11
Major	£292-0-0	£249-10-4	+£42-9-8
Captain	£211-0-0	£142-14-11	+£68-13-0
Lieutenant	£118-12-6	£53-19-5	+£64-13-1
Ensign	£95-16-3	£27-15-0	+£68-1-3

* This figure akes into account what an officer would have received in interest for the money which he paid for his commission, based upon the Regulation Prices of Commissions. It can clearly be seen that to obtain a commission without purchase was financially very desirable.

Bibliography and Sources

Unpublished Works & Manuscripts:

Blue Books, British Library.
British Parliamentary Papers on South African Affairs, British Library
Census Returns 1841–71, Gwynedd Archives, Caernarfon.
Central Library Papers, Royal Military Academy, Sandhurst.
Chelmsford Papers, National Army Museum.
Codrington Papers, National Army Museum.
Colonial Office Papers, Registers of Correspondence (Transvaal), PRO.
David Hughes Charities MSS, Gwynedd Archive Service, Llangefni.
Gelliwig Collection, National Library of Wales.
Llanfair-Brynodol Papers, National Library of Wales.
Map Department, British Library.
Misc Papers, relating to the campaign against Sekhukhuni, 1878, National Army
    Museum.
Parish Registers, Llanrug, Gwynedd Archives Service, Caernarfon.
Paymaster General Papers, Public Record Office.
Rowlands Papers, Transvaal Archives Depôt.
WO12, PRO, Muster Rolls, 41st Regiment, 1st Battalion.
WO 32, VC Records, Public Records Office.
WO32, Miscellaneous papers relating to operations in the Transvaal 1878-79, Public
    Records Office.
WO 76, Record of Officers Service, Public Records Office.
Shepstone Papers, Natal Archives.
Sir Evelyn Wood Collection, Natal Archives.
Sutton Valence School records.
Wilbraham Papers, Cheshire Record Office.

Published Books:

ALLAN, W. (Major General), *My Early Soldiering Days,* Edinburgh, 1897.
ARMSTRONG, John, *Freemasonry in Cheshire,* London, 1901.
Army List (various issues).
AYLWARD, Alfred, *The Transvaal of Today,* London, 1878.
BANCROFT, James W., *Rorke's Drift,* Spellmount, Tunbridge Wells, 1988.
BANNATYNE, -, *History of the 30th Regiment.*
BARING PEMBERTON, W., *Battles of the Crimean War,* Batsford, London, 1962.

BENTLEY, Nicholas (Editor), *Russell's Despatches from the Crimea 1854–1856*, Andre Deutsch, London, 1966.

BRACKENBURY, GEORGE, *Descriptive Sketches illustrating Mr William Simpson's drawings of the seat of war in the East*, London, 1855.

BRACKENBURY, Sir Henry, *Chief of Staff's Journal of Military Operations in the Transvaal, 1879*, HMSO.

BRERETON, J. M. & SAVORY, A. C. S., *The History of The Duke of Wellington's Regiment (West Riding) 1702–1992*, The Duke of Wellington's Regiment, Halifax, 1993.

CARY, A. D. L. & McCANCE, Stouppe, *Historical Records of the Royal Welch Fusiliers (late the 23rd Foot)*, Vol. II, 1816–1914, 1923.

CLARK, G. B., *British Policy Towards the Boers*, London, 1881.

COLENSO, Frances E. & DURNFORD, Edward (Lt Colonel), *History of the Zulu War and Its Origins*, London, 1881.

COPE, Sir William H., *History of the Rifle Brigade (the 95th)*, London, 1877.

CRESWICKE, Louis, *South Africa & the Transvaal War*, Edinburgh, 1900.

CROOK, M. J. *The Evolution of the Victoria Cross*, Ogilby Trusts, London, 1975.

EMERY, Frank, *The Red Soldier – Letters from the Zulu War*, London, 1977.

EVERETT, Sir Henry (Major General), *The Somerset Light Infantry 1685–1914*. London, 1934.

FENTON, Richard, *Tours in Wales 1804–1813*, London, 1917.

FFRENCH BLAKE, R. L. V., *The Crimean War*, Leo Cooper, London, 1971.

GRIFFITH, J. E., *Pedigrees of Anglesey and Carnarvonshire Families*, Liverpool, 1914 (reprinted 1985 and 19.

GROVES, –, *Historical Records of the 7th Royal Fusiliers*, 1903.

HAGGARD, H. Rider, *Cetawayo and His His White Neighbours*, London, 1906.

HARRISON, –, *Recollections of a Life in the British Army*, n.d.

HUME, John R., *Reminiscences of the Crimean Campaign*, London, 1894.

JONES, JOHN (MYRDDIN FARDD), *Llen Gwerin Sir Gaernarfon*, –.

JOURDAIN, H. F. N. (Lt. Colonel) & FRASER, Edward, *The Connaught Rangers*, Vol. 2, London, 1926.

KINGLAKE, A. W., *The War in the Crimea*, 1863–77.

KNIGHT, Ian, *Brave Mens' Blood — The Epic of the Zulu War, 1879*, —.

KNIGHT, Ian, *Nothing Remains But to Fight — The Defence of Rorkes Drift, 1879*, Greenwood, London, 1993.

LANGLEY, M., *The Loyal Regiment*, 1976.

LEE, A., *History of the 33rd Foot*, Jarrold, London, 1922.

LEHMANN, Joseph, *The First Boer War*, Cape, London, 1972.

LOCK, Ron, *Blood on the Painted Mountain—Zulu Victory and Defeat Hlobane and Kambula, 1879*, London, 1995

LOMAX, D. A. N., *A History of the Services of the 41st (The Welsh) Regiment*, Devonport, 1899.

MACKINNON, J. P. & SHADBOLT, S. H., *The South African Campaign of 1879*, London, 1882.

McTOY, E. D., *A Brief History of the 13th Regiment (P.A.L.I.) in South Africa During the Transvaal and Zulu Difficulties 1877–8–9*, Devonport, 1880.

Madras Army List (various issues).

MORRIS, Donald R., *The Washing of the Spears*, Cape, London, 1965.

Narrative of Field Operations connected with the Zulu War of 1878–1879, H.M.S.O., London,

NEWNHAM-DAVIS, N., *The Transvaal Under the Queen*, Sands, London, 1900.

PEARSE, H. W., *Redan Windham*, London, 1897.

PETRE, -, *The Royal Berkshire Regiment*, Vol 1, 1925.

ROBERTS, Field Marshal Sir Frederick S., *Forty-One Years in India*, London, 1897.

RUSSELL, W. H., *The War from the Landing at Gallipoli to the Death of Lord Raglan*, George Routledge, London, 1855.

STIRLING, John, *The Colonials in South Africa*, 1907.

STOTHERD, E. A. W. (Colonel), *Sabre and Saddle*.

STRUBBEN, H. W., *Recollections of Adventures Pioneering and Developing in South Africa*.

SUTHERLAND, -, *Tried and Valiant*, 1972.

TAYLOR, G. C., *Journal of Adventures with the British Army*, 1856.

TOMASSON, W. H., *With the Irregulars in the Transvaal and Zululand*, London, 1881.

VALE, Colonel W. L., *History of the South Staffordshire Regiment*.

VOYLE, Major General G. E., *A Military Dictionary*, London, 1876.

WALE, Rev. H. J., *Sword and Surplice*, 1880.

WHITEHORNE, A. C., *The History of the Welch Regiment*, Cardiff, 1932.

WILKINS, Philip A., *The History of the Victoria Cross*, London, 1904.

WILLIAMS, Rev. Hugh., *Rural Welsh Parishes*, Llithfaen, 1907.

WILLIAMS, W. Alister, *The VCs of Wales and the Welsh Regiments*, Wrexham, 1984.

WYLLY, –, *Loyal North Lancashire Regiment*, Vol. 1, 1933.

WYLLY, –, *The 95th (The Derbyshire) Regiment in the Crimea*, 1899.

WYNDHAM-SMITH, Kenneth, 'The Campaigns against the Bapedi of Sekhukhune 1877-79', *Archives Yearbook for South African History*, Vol. 1, Johannesburg, 1967.

Newspapers and Journals:

Army & Navy Gazette (various issues).

Carnarfon & Denbigh Herald (various issues).

Illustrated London News (various issues).

Journal Society for Army Historical Research (various issues).

London Gazette (various issues).

North Wales Chronicle (various issues).

Soldiers of the Queen, Vol. 6, 1980,
    WILLIAMS, W. Alister, 'Inkerman – The Opening Round'.

Times of Natal (various issues).

Transactions of the Caernarvonshire Historical Society (various issues).